Debunking Six Myths in the Ques

Get a Life

Vicki Courtney

LifeWay Press
Nashville, Tennessee

ISBN 0-6330-8890-0

This book is a resource in the Christian Growth category of the Christian Growth Study Plan. Course CG-0810

Dewey Decimal Classification: 248.843
Subject Headings: CHRISTIAN LIFE \ WOMEN

To order additional copies of this resource: WRITE LifeWay Church Resources Customer Service; One LifeWay Plaza; Nashville, TN 37234-0113; FAX order to (615) 251-5933; PHONE (800) 458-2772; EMAIL *customerservice@lifeway.com;* ORDER ONLINE at *www.lifeway.com;* or VISIT the LifeWay Christian Store serving you.

Printed in the United States of America

Editor in Chief: Dale McCleskey
Editor: Gena Rogers
Copy Editor: Beth Shive
Art Director: Jon Rodda
Illustrations: Dan Brawner

Leadership and Adult Publishing
LifeWay Church Resources
One LifeWay Plaza
Nashville, TN 37234-0175

Contents

About the Author

Vicki Courtney is the founder of Virtuous Reality Ministries and virtuousreality.com™, an online magazine for girls and women. She is a national speaker to youth, college students, and women of all ages. She is the author of *Virtuous Reality: Becoming the Ideal Woman,* a Bible study resource for college women and *The Virtuous Woman: Shattering the SuperWoman Myth,* a Bible study resource for women of all ages.

A graduate of the University of Texas at Austin, Vicki became a Christian during her junior year while attending a conference for college students. Prior to that she was strongly opposed to the Christian faith. Her life before Christ greatly influences her writing and speaking as she seeks to be sensitive to women in the body of Christ as well as to those who still seek Him.

Vicki resides in Austin, Texas, where she is a member of The Church at Canyon Creek. She enjoys occasional dates with her husband, Keith; cheering for sons, Ryan and Hayden, in their sport du jour; and shopping with her daughter, Paige.

Introduction

From the time we are young, people tell us to take control of our lives. "You are in charge of your destiny." "Make it happen." "It's yours for the taking." The ideal job, a perfect husband, kids, a house, health, wealth, on and on. Young and naïve, we believe it is possible to order our future like items on a menu. Years later we are mumbling, "This is not what I ordered!"

In John 10:10, Jesus said, " 'I have come that they may have life, and that they may have it more abundantly' " (NKJV). In spite of His bold proclamation, many Christians have settled for "just a life" rather than the abundant life Christ intended. Some wonder if it is even possible for *abundant* and *life* to appear in the same sentence. Was Jesus talking to someone else?

For years I ordered off the world's menu when it came to the abundant life. In the end, I was left yearning for something more. The Greek word for *abundantly* in John 10:10 is *perissos* (per-is-sos') which means "beyond measure, superabundant, or exceedingly abundantly above." Don't mistake the life Jesus referred to as simply abundant–it's so much more!

I took Jesus up on His offer and traded my average life for an abundant life. How about you? Are you experiencing a life that is exceedingly abundantly above, or are you settling for just a life? Join me as we take a look at six myths that hinder women in their quest for the abundant life. It's never too late. The life you've always wanted is within your reach. Don't settle for anything less. Jesus claimed it. He meant it. Now, go and … get a life!

About the Study

To get the most out of your study consider the following suggestions:

- Spend time meditating on and discussing with others what God is revealing to you.
- Trust the Holy Spirit to be your teacher. Ask Him for guidance as you study. Release your mind and heart in ready obedience to all He will teach you.
- Pray sincerely both alone and with others. Base your prayers on what the Holy Spirit has revealed to you.
- Keep a spiritual journal of God's activity in your life as well as your response to Him throughout the study. When God speaks, it is important to record it. Your memory will not always recall these "special moments," but your journal will!
- Live out your growing relationship and knowledge of God in your daily life. Share this freely with others. Expect God to honor your faithful obedience to Him.

Each week of study contains 5 days of material. You will need 15-20 minutes each day to complete your study. The learning activities will help you internalize the material. Don't skip them. They are there to challenge you and to draw application from what God has to say to you. It will also be important for you to read the related Scripture passages, even when they aren't tied to a learning activity. This will give you additional background and insight into what the Lord wants to teach you through His Word.

The resource I used for study of Greek and Hebrew words is Biblesoft's *New Exhaustive Strong's Numbers and Concordance with Expanded Greek-Hebrew Dictionary.*[1] You will find these words and definitions in italics.

You will benefit more from this study if you participate with a group of women who are also studying *Get a Life!* Small-group discussions will give you the opportunity to learn from the insights of others and will motivate you to learn more.

God bless you in your study.

---

[1] *New Exhaustive Strong's Numbers and Concordance with Expanded Greek-Hebrew Dictionary.* Biblesoft and International Bible Translators, Inc., Seattle, WA.

Week 1

Smooth Life, Cherry on Top, Hold the Pits

Myth 1: If I follow Christ, my life will be trouble free.

I remember when I got the phone call from one of my friends telling me that a mutual friend, Elizabeth, had collapsed and been rushed to the hospital. After many tests, Elizabeth was diagnosed with a brain tumor, and surgery was scheduled for the following week. The phone call was to ask all prayer warriors to pray for the surgery and, specifically, that the tumor would not be malignant. The following week Elizabeth came through the surgery, but the news was devastating. She was diagnosed with a malignant, stage IV brain tumor. She was given a life expectancy of eight to nine months.

Elizabeth and I began our friendship when my youngest child was assigned to her first grade class in 1999. Elizabeth loved Jesus more than life itself, and she passed her love for the Lord down to her students. She and her husband were committed Christians and had one young daughter. At the time she collapsed, she was doing in-service for a new teaching position in another state. One day she was facing an exciting new position and the next day she was thinking about how to spend what could be her last year in this world.

To the amazement of her doctors, Elizabeth beat the odds and survived 21 months. In my last phone conversation with Elizabeth, two weeks before she died, she expressed frustration that she had lost her ability to walk and was resigned to a wheelchair. As we ended our conversation and said good-bye for what would be the last time, she reminded me that it wouldn't be long before she could get rid of that dreaded wheelchair. In spite of her devastating circumstances, Elizabeth was a woman at peace.

Unfortunately, Christians are not exempt from adversity. Trials can come when we least expect them, often posing a threat to our quest for the abundant life. What can we do about these inevitable setbacks? This week we will look at someone in Scripture who experienced more than his fair share of trials and came out a winner in the end. What was his secret? Join me, and let's find out.

Isn't Life Grand?

When we think of Jacob's son, Joseph, likely the first thing that comes to mind is his coat of many colors. Ask anyone who has grown up going to church, "What is special about Joseph?" and you'll probably get the coat answer. From the time Joseph received the coat from Jacob, his life was never the same. One day he was the favored child of his father, sportin' a new coat. The next day his life was the pits, literally.

Joseph often tended the sheep with his half brothers, the sons of Bilhah and Zilpah. Joseph's mother, Rachel, was the favored wife of Jacob. Before marrying Rachel, Jacob had been tricked by Rachel's father into marrying her older sister, Leah. While Rachel won Jacob's heart, Leah was the one who provided him with sons.

In her desperation to provide Jacob with a son, Rachel took matters into her own hands and had her servant, Bilhah, sleep with Jacob. Bilhah provided Jacob with two sons. Leah followed by having her servant, Zilpah, sleep with Jacob to provide him with two more sons. Ten sons later, Rachel finally had a son, Joseph. She later had one more son, Benjamin, but she died during childbirth. And we thought soap operas weren't real! This one would take an award at the Daytime Emmys hands down!

Read Genesis 37:2-11. Why did Joseph's brothers hate him (v. 4)?

____

Do you think he sensed his brothers' hatred before he reported his dream to them? ❑ Yes ❑ No ❑ Maybe

Describe Joseph's first dream (v. 7). ______________________

____

How did his second dream differ from the first (v. 9)? ______________

____

The original Hebrew word for *bow* is *shachah* (shaw-khaw'), which means *to pay homage to royalty or God*. No wonder his brothers and father reacted so strongly!

Even though Jacob initially rebuked Joseph, what does verse 11 say?

____

God used the dream to hint to Joseph that He planned to use him in a mighty way. Joseph seemed to be more bent on bragging to his brothers than attempting to decipher the dream for its true meaning. Jacob, however, was a man of God and kept the matter in mind.

Think of a time when God hinted that He desired to use you in His kingdom purposes. Describe what He laid on your heart.

____

____

____

____

What action have you taken regarding what He laid on your heart?
❑ I have committed it to prayer and am waiting for direction from God.
❑ God has made Himself clear and I am following through.
❑ I blew it off. Why would He want to use me anyway?

If you were unable to recall such a time, do you believe that God desires to use you? ❑ Yes ❑ No

Read Ephesians 2:10 in the margin. Who does this verse say we are?

____

What were we created to do? ______________________________

____

Prepared by Whom? ______________________________

We are God's workmanship, created in Christ Jesus to do good works, which God prepared in advance for us to do.
–Ephesians 2:10

What is one truth you would draw from the Scripture you've studied today?

Think about it. If God prepared good works in advance for us to do, wouldn't it make sense that He would make it a priority to reveal our job assignments to us?

Read Ephesians 2:10 again, but this time say it out loud and substitute the words, "I am" and "me" for the underlined words.

As you close in prayer today, reflect on the awesome truth that God desires to use you. That God desires to use me to accomplish His kingdom purposes blows me away. What an awesome promise!

Day 2

Life Is the Pits!

We left off with Joseph sitting on top of the world. Can't you just see him? I picture him standing before his older brothers, wearing his beautiful coat, and describing his dream with a knowing and confident smirk on his face. Does life get any better than this? Somehow that saying, "Pride goes before a fall," comes to mind. Let's read on and find out what happened.

Read Genesis 37:12-20. Joseph heads out to check on his brothers. As they spot him in the distance they make a plan. What is it?

What word do they use to refer to Joseph?

The dream had not escaped their thinking. Should it be a prophecy of things to come, the brothers would take matters into their own hands. Bowing down to Joseph was not an option.

Read Genesis 37:21-24. What was Reuben's suggestion?

Of all the brothers, Reuben had more reason to hate Joseph. As the firstborn son of Jacob, he watched many privileges normally intended for the firstborn bestowed upon Joseph instead. Yet he persuaded the others to spare Joseph's life.

Read Genesis 37:25-28. What did they do before they threw him into the pit?

____

____

Joseph's coat was his badge of honor. Unfortunately, it served as a constant reminder to his brothers that he was the favored son.

How do you think Joseph reacted when he was thrown into the pit?

❑ He threatened to get the best lawyer in Canaan and take them all to court.
❑ He asked them to throw down his coat in case it got nippy at night.
❑ He begged for his life.

They said to one another, "Surely we are being punished because of our brother. We saw how distressed he was when he pleaded with us for his life, but we would not listen; that's why this distress has come upon us."
–Genesis 42:21

Read Genesis 42:21 for the answer. How would you have reacted? Remember, the pit is deep and once the perpetrators head off, the odds of someone finding you are slim to none.

What sort of new plan did the brothers hatch in Genesis 37:26-27?

____

____

Reread verse 28. Try to imagine the agony Joseph must have felt as he witnessed his brothers collect 20 shekels of silver and give him over to the Ishmaelite traders as a slave.

Verses 29-35 tell of the brothers plan to cover up their crime and Jacob's reaction to his missing son. Reuben appeared to be the only one who was sorrowful over the deed. However, it didn't stop him from participating in the cover-up.

In Genesis 37:36, we see Joseph beginning a new chapter of his life, one he never imagined would be included in his story. He had gone from a beloved and favored son of Jacob to a slave traded for 20 pieces of silver, almost overnight. He knew his brothers disliked him, but he probably never imagined they would plot to kill him or sell him into slavery.

I can't begin to imagine what must have been going through this 17-year-old boy's mind as he made the trip to Egypt with strangers. He most likely begged his captors to release him, attempting to explain his situation. He had plenty to think about as he made the long journey. No doubt, he wondered if he would ever see his father again. Did he ponder his brothers' rejection? Did he fear the future, wondering what would become of him once he arrived in Egypt? Did he cry out to his God, the God of Abraham, Isaac, and his father, Jacob? If he did cry out to God, did he question the meaning of his dreams? Surely this was not part of the plan! It didn't add up!

When did you last experience an unforeseen trial? ______________________

____

What was the situation? ______________________

____

____

What is one truth you would draw from the Scripture you've studied today?

____

____

____

____

How did you react to the trial? ______________________

____

____

What was your attitude regarding God at the time?

- ❑ I'm not surprised this happened. I'm not one of God's favorites.
- ❑ God, are you there?
- ❑ God, if You love me, how can You allow this to happen?
- ❑ God, only with Your help can I get through this trial.

The abundant life is possible, even in the face of adversity.

As you close in prayer today, ask God to build your faith that you can experience the abundant life, even in the face of adversity. Claim this truth and thank Him for it.

Just When You Thought Things Couldn't Get Worse

Our story picks up with Joseph as a slave of Potiphar, an officer of the Pharaoh. Genesis 39:2 may be the most critical verse in the story of Joseph's life.

Read Genesis 39:1-2 and fill in the blanks below.

"The Lord was ________________ Joseph and he ________________."

Every step of the way God was with Joseph. Look back at the trial you described at the end of day 2. Did you ever doubt that God was with you? I believe that this truth alone transformed Joseph's life somewhere along the way to Egypt. He experienced a crisis of belief. *Is the God I've heard about all these years really concerned about my welfare?*

We will all face trials, and when we do a crisis of belief will occur. Many times we are so busy trying to find a way out of the trial, we fail to remember that God is right by our side. In addressing the notion of divine control, Oswald Chambers said, "Notion your mind with the idea that God is there. If once the mind is notioned along that line, then when you are in difficulties it is as easy as breathing to remember–Why, my Father knows all about it! It is not an effort, it comes naturally when perplexities press. Before, you used to go to this person and that, but now the notion of the Divine control is forming so powerfully in you that you go to God about it."[1]

The Lord was with Joseph and he prospered, and he lived in the house of his Egyptian master.
–Genesis 39:2

So many of us lean on people and things that we fail to lean on the One Who can carry us through. If you aren't feeling hopeful enough knowing the Lord is with you in times of trial, look again at Genesis 39:2 (in the margin). The original Hebrew word for *prosper*, is *tsalach* (tsaw-lakh') which means to *push forward.*

Have you ever experienced the kind of trial that knocks the wind out of you? The kind where you awaken in the morning and in your first groggy moments the reality of the trial floods your mind? I have, and it takes great effort just to get out of bed and keep on breathing. Yet, with the awesome knowledge that the Lord is with me comes the ability to push forward.

With the awesome knowledge that the Lord is with us comes the ability to push forward.

Joseph pushed forward because he knew God was with him. Does this mean he forgot his trial and felt no sadness or pain? Absolutely not. He simply rested in the fact that though his circumstances seemed out of control, his God was not. Many of us have a head knowledge of this truth, but it hasn't taken root in our hearts. When it does, watch out! It is truly life-changing.

In the margin, list some trials that you or someone you know have experienced that would fall into the "knock the wind out of you" category.

How might the simple truth that God is with us and desires to prosper us offer hope in the midst of such trials? Write your thoughts on the lines below.

____

____

Of what did Potiphar put Joseph in charge in Genesis 39:3-10?

____

Why did God begin to bless Potiphar?______________________

____

When Potiphar's wife attempted to seduce Joseph, what was his response? What does he say to her regarding his God?

____

____

Verse 9 gives us insight into Joseph's attitude toward God during this time in his life. Given his circumstances, Joseph had every reason to wonder if his God had abandoned him. It is not uncommon for people who are hurting to want to give up. Let us not forget that Joseph was a normal young man, susceptible to the same temptations as young men today. We are not told if he was tempted by her advances, but it is clear that he viewed the offense as something wicked and against God.

In spite of Joseph's stand for righteousness, Potiphar's wife betrayed Joseph and falsely accused him of trying to rape her (see Gen. 39:11-20). As a result, Potiphar had him thrown into prison.

Just when Joseph's life was beginning to look up, it took another turn for the worse. Was this his reward for putting God first and doing the right thing? The irony is that had he succumbed to the advances of Potiphar's wife, he might still have had his freedom. Regardless, Joseph did the right thing and suffered for the sake of staying true to God.

Can you think of a time when you were falsely accused of something?
❑ Yes ❑ No
How did it make you feel?____________________________________

What was the outcome? ____________________________________

____

What part did God play in the outcome? ________________________

As you wrap up today's study, reflect on the awesome truth that the Lord is with you, no matter what comes your way. Pray that this truth will become as natural as breathing.

What is one truth you would draw from the Scripture you've studied today?

____

____

____

____

Day 4

Keep on Keeping on

I can only imagine what Joseph must have been thinking as he pondered his circumstances in prison. Let's take an inventory of Joseph's trials to date:

- Rejected and betrayed at the hands of his brothers
- Thrown into a pit to die
- Sold as a slave for 20 pieces of silver
- Abducted from his father and his homeland
- Served as a slave
- Falsely accused of rape
- Thrown in prison for a crime he did not commit

Genesis 39:21-23 doesn't tell us how much time transpired between Joseph's first day in prison and his eventual position as right-hand man to the prison warden. It most likely didn't happened overnight. Once again, Joseph rested in the assurance that his God was with him and would prevail in the end.

Recently I suffered a trial that hurt me deeply. What made this trial especially difficult was that it came at the hands of someone I trusted. For several days I moped around in my jammies and fluffy slippers with a big bag of chips tucked under my arm, mumbling, "Why me, God? Why is this happening to me?"

I knew God had called me into His service. I had been walking in light of this truth and out of nowhere came a setback. Why would God allow this untimely interruption in His kingdom work? It didn't make sense. Did I cry out to God in my hurt and frustration? You bet I did! … in between all the phone calls I made to friends to rehash the details. After all, isn't that what a pity party is all about?

Like Joseph, somewhere in the middle of that very painful trial, I experienced a crisis of belief. Either God is with me or He isn't. If He is with me, I can rest assured that He knows my hurt and disappointment. I can also rest assured that He is aware of my situation and desires to work good from it. I chose to acknowledge His presence and asked forgiveness for not doing so sooner.

When was the last time you had a pity party? ____________________

Write about the circumstances in the margin.

Let me add a disclaimer that pity parties in and of themselves are not wrong. God does not expect us to face adversity alone and often uses others to speak His wisdom and administer comfort. The key is putting God first on the guest list. When God is first, we have a tendency to run the rest of the guest list past Him and make sure it meets His approval before sending out the invitation(s).

Had I acknowledged God sooner in my time of adversity, my guest list would have been cut down to a couple of trusted Christian friends. Looking to others for comfort can act as a temporary salve when dressing our wounds, but it will not take the place of the healing touch of God.

In regard to the pity party you listed above, where was God on your guest list?

❑ I meant to include Him, but somehow I overlooked His name.
❑ He was first on my list. I called Him before calling anyone else.
❑ Whoops. Is He still at the same address?

How did God use Joseph in the lives of the Pharaoh's chief cup-bearer and chief baker according to Genesis 40:1-18?

____

____

Once again, we are not sure how much time has passed since Joseph entered prison. Chapter 40 opens "some time later," so it is clear that Joseph spent his fair share of days in prison by the time the cup-bearer and baker arrived. Verse 4 indicates that even more time elapsed between the incarceration of the two men and their dreams.

What does Joseph say to the two men in verse 8?

____

What is the one thing Joseph asks of the cup-bearer in verse 14?

____

How does he describe his situation in verse 15? ________________

____

According to Genesis 40:20-23, Joseph's interpretations were right on target. The cup-bearer was restored to his original position, but the baker lost his life. Yet, in spite of Joseph's kindness, the cup-bearer did not remember him to the Pharaoh.

Imagine that you are Joseph. Your one big shot rests on the shoulders of a man you helped. Now it all makes sense! God will use this man as His instrument to plead your case before the Pharaoh. This is all part of God's plan!

You can almost taste the freedom. Your heart pounds every time you hear footsteps coming toward the prison. Any day now, someone should come bearing news that the Pharaoh will hear your case. Days go by, months, a year, but nothing. You are sure you have been forgotten. If the cup-bearer didn't remember you in the early days after his release, what would cause him to remember you now? Imagine Joseph's despair.

Have you ever done something for someone who later failed to show gratitude and eventually forgot you altogether? ❑ Yes ❑ No If yes, how did it make you feel?

____

____

What is one truth you would draw from the Scripture you've studied today?

Have you ever felt like God has forgotten you? ❑ Yes ❑ No
Have you ever mistakenly put your trust or hope in a person to deliver you and they failed to come through? ❑ Yes ❑ No

Read Genesis 41:1-13. What caused the cup-bearer to finally remember Joseph?

Joseph had his one big chance (see Gen. 41:14-16), yet he gave 100 percent of the credit to God. After spending two more years in prison after the cup-bearer was released, Joseph could have easily believed that God had forgotten him. His response to the Pharaoh indicates that he continued to have confidence that his God was with him and would work good from his situation.

What was the result of Joseph interpreting the Pharaoh's dream correctly in Genesis 41:17-45?

List some of the perks Joseph received in his new job? (vv. 39-44)

My favorite is verse 43, "He had him ride in a chariot as his second-in-command, and men shouted before him, 'Make way!' " The word used for *make way* is *'abrek* (ab-rake'), which means *to kneel or bow the knee.* I like to imagine Joseph sitting in his grand chariot and his men shouting to the crowd, "Bow the knee, bow the knee."

What sweet justice to watch Potiphar, Potiphar's wife, and the cup-bearer bow the knee as his chariot passes by. Knowing Joseph, it didn't matter to him that others who once treated him with ill-respect were now at his mercy. Joseph's God prevailed and he was finally free. Things were looking up for Joseph. Little did he know, it would only get better.

In closing, reflect on a crisis of belief in your life. Thank God for that time and what He taught you through the crisis. Ask Him to help you never lose sight of Who is in control, no matter what the circumstances.

No Pain, No Gain

We pick up with Joseph travelling throughout Egypt, implementing his strategy for storing the grain during the seven years of plenty. As part of the new job benefits, the Pharaoh gave Joseph a wife, Asenath, daughter of Potiphera, priest of On. The priests were considered the highest and most privileged class in Egypt. Intermarriage with a daughter of a priest sealed your social position in the land.

As predicted, the 7 years of plenty occurred, followed by 7 years of famine. Joseph's family of origin began to feel the pangs of hunger. Jacob had heard rumor of grain in Egypt and sent 10 of his sons to buy food. Benjamin, the youngest, remained with Jacob. Joseph would finally come face-to-face with his brothers after all these years.

When Joseph's brothers arrived in Egypt, the 7 years of prosperity had come to an end, so it had been approximately 20-22 years since he last saw his brothers.

When they came face-to-face, what did his brothers do? (Gen. 42:6)

____

Reread Genesis 37:5-8. Did Joseph's dream come true? ❑ Yes ❑ No

What began as a hint from God when Joseph was 17 years old was fully realized 22 years later. With his brothers bowing before him, Joseph recognized them and recalled the dream. He didn't give his identity away and spoke harshly to his brothers, accusing them of being spies. His objective was to find out how his father, Jacob, and brother, Benjamin, were doing. After incarcerating his brothers for 3 days, he brought them out of prison and informed them that one brother would have to stay behind while the others returned to get their youngest brother and bring him back. Genesis 42:21-24 tells us what transpired next.

Even after 22 years, it caused Joseph great sadness to recall the day he was thrown into the pit. Time had perhaps taken the edge off the pain, but the day he spent in the pit would never be erased from his mind.

Can you recall an incident or trial that occurred long ago but still impacts you today? Unfortunately, I can think of more than one. I felt great sadness as I read Joseph's response, yet at the same time I felt relieved that Joseph was no different from you or me. His brothers' very presence served as a painful reminder of their rejection. Unbeknownst to them, they were now dependent on the very life they had at one time attempted to extinguish.

Joseph detained Simeon and sent the rest of his brothers back with grain to feed their families. They were to return with Benjamin. The brothers returned to the land of Canaan and told Jacob of the man who gave them grain and kept their brother, Simeon, until they could return with Benjamin. Jacob insisted that he could not let Benjamin go, as he recalled the loss of Joseph.

Once the grain ran out, there remained no other choice but to return to Egypt to purchase more grain. Judah was able to finally convince Jacob that Benjamin must come with them on the trip and assumed personal responsibility for his well-being. Jacob relented and sent them on their way.

Why does Joseph excuse himself according to Genesis 43:24-31?
❑ To pay his compliments to the chef
❑ He couldn't stand the sight of his brothers
❑ He was overcome with emotion at the sight of Benjamin

Once again we see a very human side to Joseph. Not only did Benjamin not take part in the scheme to kill Joseph, he was Joseph's only full brother. After dinner, Joseph again sent them on their way with more grain, but instructed his steward to plant his silver cup in Benjamin's bag. Joseph sent his steward after his brothers to search their bags.

The steward caught up with the brothers and accused them of stealing the cup. Upon searching their bags, the silver cup was found in Benjamin's bag and the brothers returned to the city. The penalty? Benjamin was to remain as a servant. Upon hearing this, the brothers pleaded their innocence before Joseph and begged for his mercy. Finally, the games came to an end and Joseph revealed his identity to his brothers.

In Genesis 45:1-15 we read that the brothers returned to share the news with Jacob. The entire family relocated to Egypt. So many trials, yet God prevailed in the end. Great insight into Joseph comes with the meaning of the names given to his two sons.

Read Genesis 41:50-52. What did the name of Joseph's first son mean?

____

Joseph did not completely forget his troubles or his father's household. God helped take his mind off these things as Joseph grew in the knowledge that his God was with him.

What did the name of Joseph's second son mean?

____

Joseph gave control over to God when ordering his life. As a result, God caused him to be fruitful in spite of great suffering.

Joseph had a choice when it came to his response to adversity. How would he emerge from the pit? from rejection? from betrayal? from a life of slavery? from prison? Would he become bitter or better? Joseph chose better because Joseph chose God.

As you reflect of today's study, ask yourself these questions: *Have I experienced something that I would consider a "land of suffering"? Did I emerge from it bitter or better?*

What is one truth you would draw from the Scripture you've studied today?

____

____

____

____

Truth to Go

As believers, our lives will not be trouble free, but God promises to be with us. And He desires to work good in all we experience. Will you trust Him with control of your life? Allow Joseph's story to transform you. The abundant life is only possible when God is in control. When adversity comes your way (and it will come), you will have a choice to make just like Joseph did. Choose better instead of bitter; choose God!

---

[1] Oswald Chambers, *My Utmost for His Highest* (New York: Dodd, Mead & Company, 1935), July 16.

Week 2

One Prince Charming, Well-Done Please

Myth #2: A man will make me happy.

"Off to the palace went Cinderella in the king's coach, with the happy grand duke by her side. The prince was delighted to see her again, and so was his father, the king. This sweet and beautiful girl won the hearts of all who met her. In no time at all she was princess of the land. And she and her husband, the charming prince, rode to their palace in a golden coach to live … happily ever after."

I remember hearing the Cinderella tale and wondering if there was such a thing as Prince Charming. I dreamed of the day my long-awaited prince would ride into town (in my dream he was driving a black Porsche), declare his undying love for me, and sweep me off my feet. Little did I know, I would date quite a few Prince Anything-but-Charmings before I would finally meet my prince.

I met my prince in 1985, but he had little in common with the guy in my fairy tale. My prince showed up in a harvest gold Mustang hatchback. Rather than sweep me off my feet, he asked me for a friend's phone number the first month I knew him. Finally, it became clear that I was his one true princess and we married in 1987. Mission accomplished. I had snagged my man and now my life would be complete … or would it?

A few years into my marriage I was still living in fairy tale la-la land, having adopted the notion that my husband had a personal responsibility to make me happy. When I placed this heavy burden on his shoulders, he eventually buckled under the weight. Where was the strikingly handsome Prince Charming I had conjured up in my childhood fantasies? Sure, he had the strikingly handsome part down, but my Prince Charming was not supposed to belch, channel surf, or leave his dirty socks on the floor for me to pick up. Maybe his mother never read him the Cinderella story.

Whether you are married or single, a man will not make you happy. This week let's do away with our silly notions of Prince Charming rescuing us from a life otherwise destined for the doldrums. Fortunately, God's plan does include a Prince, a rescue mission, and even an ending that reads, "happily ever after."

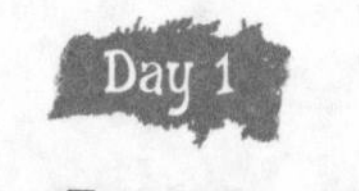

Complete Love

It was an overnight phenomenon. In 1996 single women were lining up to get the controversial book *The Rules: Time-Tested Secrets for Capturing the Heart of Mr. Right.* Authors Ellen Fein and Sherrie Schneider offered a foolproof formula for snagging a man with 35 time-tested secrets. Rules included: Don't call him, end the date first, and don't accept a Saturday night date after Wednesday. The success of the first book led to a second book in 1997 called *The Rules II: More Rules to Live and Love by.* As long as books were selling, Mrs. Fein and Mrs. Schneider would keep penning their words of wisdom and offering their seminars throughout the country.

Book number three released in May, 2001 under the title *The Rules for Marriage: Time-Tested Secrets for Making Your Marriage Work.* However, before the finished product hit the bookstore shelves, word leaked out that after 16 years of marriage, Ellen Fein and her husband were divorcing. *The Rules* books would become garage sale fodder overnight. While Ms. Fein was busy writing the manuscript of a marriage book, her own marriage was crumbling. Hmm. Sorry, Ms. Fein, but I'll pass on the marriage advice.

Why do you think women buy into gimmicks like this?

I must admit to a time in my life when *The Rules* books might have been on my reading list. My mother did a fine job reinforcing the mantra that "a man will not make you happy." Unfortunately, try as she did, her words rang hollow. By the time I got to high school, I was already brainwashed by the fairy tales with perfect princes and the romance novels with main characters who rescue their damsels in distress.

I bought into the snag-a-man tactics of the teen magazines and attended one too many movies that left me swiping away tears of romantic joy. Ahhhh, yes, my time would come and I, too, would meet the man who would complete me. We would walk the sandy beaches hand-in-hand with the sun setting on the ocean and live happily ever after.

My first several years of wedded bliss didn't quite follow the Cinderella script. My chariot was a minivan. The castle needed cleaning. The prince and our little subjects needed feeding. When bedtime rolled around I would collapse into the bed and mumble something to the effect of, "Touch me and prepare to die." Reality had set in. Still I was hopeful that the proverbial "happily ever after" lingered somewhere on the landscape of the future. Wasn't marriage part of the equation for the abundant life?

My husband, Keith, is an excellent husband and father. He has gained a reputation at work and church for being a man of godly wisdom and integrity. He is about as perfect as any man gets. No doubt, he's the better half of our marriage. Yet, try as he may, he fell short of providing me with the complete happiness I longed for.

Do you think a happy marriage is an important factor in the quest for the abundant life? ❑ Yes ❑ No Why or why not?

____

____

What are some expectations you have (or have had in the past) of a husband? Check all that apply.

❑ He will complete me.
❑ He will be my best friend, and we will share our innermost thoughts.
❑ He will possess an uncanny ability to read my mind.
❑ I will often catch him staring at me with open adoration.
❑ When I'm talking he will listen, nodding in agreement.
❑ He will sense when I am stressed and try to help.
❑ Others (list your own in the margin)

If you checked all of the above, I suggest you head to the nearest animal shelter and get a dog! It isn't fair to place such unrealistic expectations on a man. Unfortunately, I learned this the hard way. My goal in this week's session is not to bash men or the institution of marriage, but rather to encourage women to think outside the normal stereotypes that often link snagging a man or marriage to the abundant life.

Which category do you fall into? Check one.

❑ I can't imagine the abundant life is possible without a man.
❑ I can't imagine the abundant life is possible with a man.
❑ Married or single, I can have an abundant life.

In the movie, *Jerry Maguire,* Tom Cruise plays a talent scout who places his career above his marriage and eventually separates from his wife. In the end, he recognizes the error of his ways and jumps on an airplane to patch things up with his wife. When he walks through the door of his home, he finds his wife and a multitude of her friends gathered in the living room. He nervously delivers a beautiful and dramatic monologue and ends it with, "I love you. You complete me." She responds with, "You had me at hello." I wanted to scream, "You go, girl! You found your man!"

My God will meet all your needs according to his glorious riches in Christ Jesus.
–Philippians 4:19

In the margin circle what Philippians 4:19 says God will do. Underline how God will do it.

This often quoted verse reminds us that God knows we have needs, and He desires to meet them. We often misunderstand this verse because our perceived needs differ from our actual needs.

Read Ephesians 1:22-23 and Colossians 2:9-10. Circle the words *fill, fullness,* or *complete* every time you see them.

Christ possesses the fullness of whom? ______________________

In whom have you been given fullness? ______________________

What is His position? ______________________

What is one truth you would draw from the Scripture you've studied today?

____

____

____

____

Interestingly, the actual Greek word for each of the words listed above is *pleroo* (play-ro'-o), which means *to level up (a hollow), or to finish or complete.* Only God has the ability to complete us and He does so with the fullness of His Son. There's not another man alive who can complete us.

End today by asking God to level up the hollow places in your life and complete you according to His riches in Christ Jesus.

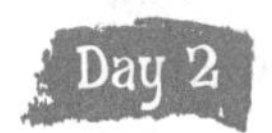

Perfect Love

I remember the first time I received proclamations of love from someone who wasn't related to me. It was my third-grade Valentine's party. I could hardly wait to open the decorated shoebox filled with candy and valentines when I got home. Reading the messages on the valentines was more thrilling than eating the candy (probably a girl thing). As I pulled them out one-by-one, most of them contained the standard valentine clichés with a simple signature. That is, until I got to Gary's. Gary was a quiet, somewhat distant boy. As I looked at his homemade valentine, I could hardly believe my eyes. He must have spent hours cutting and pasting this masterpiece together.

Inside was a poem that said something like, "Roses are red, violets are blue …" I don't really remember how he ended this original sonnet, but I do remember how he signed it. It simply said, "I'm in love with you---From, Gary." Wow, someone was in love with me! I had never spoken two words to this boy, yet somehow he was in love with me. Of course, we never acknowledged the valentine and the next day we were back to the business of being third graders, more concerned with breaking through the Red Rover chain at recess.

I didn't feel that familiar flutter in my heart again until fifth grade, when a boy in my class slipped me a note that simply said, "I love you. Will you go with me? Circle yes or no." I circled yes and my heart skipped a beat as I passed the note back to him. For the rest of the year we would hardly speak, but it didn't matter–someone loved me.

As the years progressed, I experienced many episodes that caused my heart to flutter and beat peacefully for a time, with a quiet assurance that I was loved. As I progressed in this game called love, I also experienced episodes that left my heart broken and battered. By the time I got to college, the casualties were high. This love business was not all it was cracked up to be. There were expectations and strings attached to the price of love. Would I ever find my one, perfect love?

Describe a time you risked loving someone and your heart was broken.

____

____

It may have been a parent who failed to extend affection. Perhaps you witnessed your parent's divorce or a divorce of your own. Maybe a friend betrayed you or your husband walked out on you. It could be flashbacks of promiscuity that have left a residue of shame. You may have been involved in a relationship where you were abused.

One of the most painful situations happens when a marriage partner claims to no longer love his or her spouse. The pain multiplies if the partner committed adultery and claims to now love someone else. I can't imagine the rejection and pain. No wonder some women are afraid to ever love again.

Can you think of a time when you were afraid to love? ❑ Yes ❑ No

What were you afraid of? ________________________________

____

What gives us confidence on the day of judgment according to 1 John 4:17-18?

____

What will cast out fear? ________________________________

If His love made complete in our own lives gives us confidence to face judgment day, what can it offer us in regard to our earthly relationships? The unfailing love of God says, "I will love you perfectly, completely, and without error."

May your unfailing love
be my comfort,
according to your promise
to your servant.
–Psalm 119:76

Circle what God's unfailing love provides according to Psalm 119:76.

Describe a time when you were comforted by His unfailing love.

____

____

Women drive the demand for romance novels, soap operas, and romantic movies. We have an insatiable desire to be wooed, charmed, and loved intensely by someone. If this need is not being met in our lives, we try to live vicariously through made-up characters.

Read these passages and note the phrases that speak to you of love.

Psalm 139:17-18 ____________________

Isaiah 54:10____________________

Zepheniah 3:17____________________

Romans 8:37-39 ____________________

Ephesians 3:16-19____________________

1 John 3:1 ____________________

The more I study God's Word, the more amazed I am at how much God loves me. The Bible is the greatest romance novel on the market. Nothing is more beautiful than the story of redemption. It penetrates my innermost being and can evoke more emotion than a greeting card commercial, a romance novel, or an "I love you," whispered softly by my husband. The more familiar I become with the truths of this great love story, the more satisfied I become with God's perfect, unfailing love.

Understanding the unfailing love of God is critical in the quest for the abundant life.

Do you take the Bible personally? ❑ Yes ❑ No In your opinion, why don't women recognize the Bible as the greatest love story ever told?

____

End today by reading aloud Psalm 36:7-9. List below what appears on God's menu of unfailing love.

We will feast on ____________________.

We will drink ____________________.

For dessert, He offers the fountain of ____________________.

Understanding the unfailing love of God is critical in the quest for the abundant life.

What is one truth you would draw from the Scripture you've studied today?

____

____

____

____

Unconditional Love

Who can forget the final, poignant scene in *Titanic?* With room for only one person on the floating debris in the cold waters of the Atlantic, Jack allows his beloved new girlfriend the spot on the precarious board as he desperately hangs on beside her in the water. His lips blue from the cold and his voice quivering, he labors his last words and implores her to go on living without him. Finally, he is overtaken by hypothermia and Rose lets go of his hand, watching him sink below the surface. He dies for his beloved. How noble. How chivalrous.

Now, let's say that Rose wrongs or betrays Jack prior to the sinking of the ship. In spite of that fact, he forgives her and tells her that he still loves her. However, she responds with indifference, unbelief, or even indignation. Now, fast forward to the floating debris. Do you think Jack would still die for Rose? It's a rare thing for a person to die for someone they love, but you'd be hard pressed to find a person who would die for someone who has wronged them.

Read Romans 5:8 and fill in the blanks below.

"But __________ demonstrates his own __________ for us in this:

While we were ___________ sinners, Christ ___________ for us."

Jesus died for us in spite of the fact we're wretched sinners. Within the heart of every woman is the desire to hear someone say, "I will love you no matter what. I will love you when you are unlovable. I will love you when you don't measure up to my expectations. I will love you for who you are instead of what you do." We desire to be loved unconditionally, no strings attached.

We desire to be loved unconditionally, no strings attached.

Do you have the capacity to love unconditionally? ❑ Yes ❑ No

Some people may come close, but no human is capable of loving another with a perfect, unconditional love.

Years ago I saw a skit that forever impacted my life. The first scene began with a family who had adopted a 17-year-old son after losing their teenage daughter to a drunk driver. They took the boy into their home and lavished their love on him. We come to find out that the son they adopted is the drunk driver who killed their daughter. Rather then allow him to be convicted and sent to prison, they rescued him and adopted him into their own family. They loved him as they loved their daughter. He was given a second chance. He was forgiven. He was redeemed.

The skit powerfully made the obvious point that we are no different than the drunk driver in the skit. Our sinful actions have caused the death of our Father's beloved Son. Rather than suffer the penalty for our actions, He gave us another chance. Further, the Father adopts us into His family and lavishes His love upon us. We are redeemed.

Read Colossians 1:11-14. From what did God rescue us? (v. 13)

____

Read Titus 3:3-7. What does verse 7 say we might become?

____

Read Ephesians 1:4-11. What do you feel when you meditate on verse 5?

____

Read Psalms 40:1-2 and 103:2-5 in the margin. In each passage, underline what God delivers us from and circle what He delivers us to.

I waited patiently for
the Lord;
he turned to me and
heard my cry.
He lifted me out of the
slimy pit,
out of the mud and mire;
he set my feet on a rock
and gave me a firm
place to stand.
–Psalm 40:1-2

Praise the Lord,
O my soul,
and forget not all
his benefits–
who forgives all your sins
and heals all your
diseases,
who redeems your life
from the pit
and crowns you with
love and compassion,
who satisfies your desires
with good things
so that your youth is
renewed like the eagle's.
–Psalm 103:2-5

If you are looking for a knight in shining armor coming to the rescue of his maiden in distress, your search is over. It doesn't get any better than this. The most beautiful love story on earth is the story of redemption. Ask David. Ask the Samaritan woman. Ask the Shunamite woman. Ask Paul. Ask me. I was originally rescued from the pit in 1985, but I'm ashamed to say that years later, as a believer, I jumped right back in. It didn't take long for the fun to wear off and the misery to set in. In desperation, I cried out to God. What followed was a rescue mission that tops anything you've ever seen on a movie screen or read in a romance novel.

All I had to do was cry out for help, place my hand in His, and allow Him to lift me out of the pit. He had been there all along, just waiting for the opportunity to rescue me. Before setting my feet on a rock, He held me close to His heart and whispered sweet somethings in my ear. He gave me a firm place to stand and crowned me with love and compassion.

I wouldn't be in ministry today had it not been for that dramatic rescue mission years ago. I just can't shut up about His love. I'm no different than the drunk driver in the skit. I deserve His wrath, yet He adopted me into His family and showers me with His perfect, unconditional love. I just don't get it. Rather than experience the penalty of death, He gave me life, and an abundant one at that.

Can you think of a time (other than your salvation) when God rescued you from the pit? Are you currently in the pit? If yes, what do you want to say to God? On a separate sheet of paper or in your prayer journal, write your thoughts in the form of a letter to God. Talk to Him from your heart.

What is one truth you would draw from the Scripture you've studied today?

____

____

____

____

For the drunk driver, the amount of liquor consumed before the accident was of little relevance. The same is true when it comes to the sin(s) we commit. Regardless of whether it was a big sin or a little sin, the result was the same. It was enough to send our Savior to the cross.

Close today by praying and thanking God for rescuing you from the pit and crowning you with love and compassion.

Everlasting Love

You also were included in Christ when you heard the word of truth, the gospel of your salvation. Having believed, you were marked in him with a seal, the promised Holy Spirit, who is a deposit guaranteeing our inheritance until the redemption of those who are God's possession–to the praise of his glory.
–Ephesians 1:13-14

Each Sunday I love to look in the newspaper at the wedding announcements. The brides-to-be all look so happy! Unfortunately, 40 percent of the smiles will fade when the marriage ends in divorce. While there are no guarantees when it comes to love between two people, Christians can rest assured that God's perfect love is lasting and eternal.

In day 2 we saw how God's perfect love never fails. In day 3 we explored God's unconditional love. Today we will see how God's perfect love is eternal. When we begin a relationship with God, we can count on the fact that He's in it for the long haul. He will not leave us, change His mind, or replace us with someone else. Once His covenant is established in our lives through Christ, it is sealed and irrevocable.

Ephesians 1:13-14 (in the margin) explains that believers are marked with a seal. What is that seal? ______________________________

Because we are prone to sin, we may at some point distance ourselves from God. Just like couples in the paper celebrating 50+ years of marriage, I want to log many years building a close relationship with my Father, through His Son, Jesus Christ.

Read Romans 8:29. God conforms us in likeness to ________________.

Read Psalm 136. What phrase appears at the end of each verse?

____

Which verses spoke most to your heart? ____________________________

The Hebrew word for *forever* is `owlam (o-lawm'), which means *time out of mind (past or future) or eternity.* God's love is eternal and continues past our earthly stay. Where human love ends, God's love will continue. As my kids would say, it will go on for "kazillion times infinity." In spite of this fact, a majority of people will invest more energy in their earthly relationships than a relationship with Jesus Christ.

Where human love ends, God's love will continue.

In your opinion, why do most people invest their energy in human relationships rather than a relationship with Jesus?

____

____

How much time do you spend with God each day in prayer, reading His

Word, Bible study, church, or other forms of worship? ________________

Are you satisfied with the amount of time you spend with God each day?
❑ Yes ❑ No If no, what can you do to change it?

____

____

We all have times when our relationship to Christ takes a back seat to other things. Sometimes we can go days, weeks, even months without seeking God through His Word or prayer.

How do you feel during times when you fail to make time with God a priority?

- ❑ No different. God knows I will call when I need Him.
- ❑ Things feel somewhat distant. It's hard to get reacquainted when I recommit to the relationship.
- ❑ I'm too preoccupied with other things to think about it.
- ❑ Hey, haven't you heard of grace?

I wonder what percentage of the marriages that end in divorce end because the couple stops communicating. It is difficult to love a person unless you know the person's likes and dislikes. It is difficult to know a person unless you talk to the person. If we fail to talk or spend time together, the relationship suffers; so does our relationship with God.

Based on your knowledge of successful relationships, what advice would you give to a new bride regarding good communication habits? (ex: be a good listener)

____

Successful relationships are the result of hard work and commitment over time.

Successful relationships don't happen overnight. Successful relationships are the result of hard work and commitment over time.

How might the communication habits you listed above help you in your relationship with God?

____

Which of these communication habits might you need to improve in your relationship with God?

____

The book of Hosea is a beautiful story of God's patient love regarding wayward Israel. Read Hosea 2:1-13. What similarities do you see between Israel's waywardness toward God and ours?

____

____

Read Hosea 2:14-20. What does God say He will do in response to wayward Israel?

____

____

When we develop a relationship with God through His Son, how long does He plan to stick it out in the relationship? __________ If you are wayward, how long will He stick it out? __________ Can any person guarantee you that kind of love? ❑ Yes ❑ No

What is one truth you would draw from the Scripture you've studied today?

____

____

____

____

Though God loves us with an eternal and everlasting love, we should never take it for granted. We should never assume that God has an obligation to love us. Quite the contrary, the Creator of the Universe chooses to love us and expects us to respond by loving Him in return. God's love is unfailing, unconditional, and eternal. You won't find a man alive who can ever match that.

Close in prayer and thank God for His eternal and everlasting love. Express your gratitude to Him for betrothing you to Him forever.

Happily-Ever-After Love

In celebration of our ninth wedding anniversary in 1996, my husband and I sat in our car in a grocery store parking lot, reminiscing over the past 11 years we had known each other. I know it doesn't sound very romantic, but this was not your average parking lot. Almost 11 years prior, in August, 1985, I was beginning my junior year at the University of Texas. I had grown weary of the party scene. A friend invited me to attend a retreat for college students over the weekend. My friend had recently found religion and no doubt thought my soul needed saving. I convinced my roommate to join me and agreed to meet my friend and his buddies in a parking lot to follow them to the retreat.

You guessed it, we met them in the same parking lot my husband and I sat in almost 11 years later. At the time, my motive in attending the retreat was to meet nicer guys. You know, the church-going type. I had recently come off a long and bitter relationship where I had even declined a proposal of marriage. Like most college girls, I longed to meet the one man who would complete me.

When my friend got there with his buddies, I immediately noticed his extremely handsome roommate. The more I visited with my friend's roommate, the more I liked him. He was self-confident, bright, and witty–even charming. I couldn't help but wonder if this was "the one." He seemed so perfect.

Yet, later at the retreat I met Someone who took my breath away. As the speaker shared about Jesus Christ, I felt a peace settle in my heart. Could this be the love I had searched for my entire life? Could Jesus fill the void in my heart? I arrived at the retreat hoping to meet a man and I left having met the Man of my dreams. As I embarked on this new journey called Christianity, my bruised heart began to heal. I would also marry my friend's charming roommate a year and a half later.

As my husband and I sat in the parking lot reflecting on our original meeting and the following 11 years, we were overcome with emotion. We have experienced our share of ups and downs. Unfortunately, in the early years of my marriage there were times I placed a greater focus on my relationship with my husband and children than my relationship with my Lord and Savior. It eventually became clear that no mortal man, including my near perfect husband, could quench the desire in my heart to be loved completely. It was then that I reflected on the Man I met in 1985. The only Man who could complete me. I renewed my vows to my Savior and fell in love with Him.

In the early years, I was guilty of knowing *about* the Lord rather than *knowing* Him. In my renewed relationship to Christ, I would dive into His Word with eagerness and relish the love story of redemption. I would rush to His feet each day to share my innermost thoughts. He became my everything.

Read Psalm 73:25. Do you desire God more than anything on earth?
❑ Yes ❑ No If God is not your everything, do you want Him to be?
❑ Yes ❑ No If so, write a prayer in the margin expressing your desire.

Read Romans 8:38-39. What can separate us from the love of God? ______

How does the passage say God shows His love toward us?

______

______

Jesus is the Author of the abundant life. Without Him, your life will be incomplete. Have you met your one perfect Love, Jesus Christ?
❑ Yes ❑ No If yes, briefly describe your introduction.

____

____

____

What is one truth you would draw from the Scripture you've studied today?

____

____

____

____

If you have not met your one perfect Love, consider doing so. Express your desire to know Him; acknowledge His death on the cross as a sacrifice for your sins; and ask Him to reside in your heart. Share your decision with someone who can help you grow and develop your new relationship.

Truth to Go

When we become Christians, we enter into the only relationship that matters for eternity. We have a responsibility to nurture and build the relationship. Jesus can do nothing more to prove His love to us. He did it all on the cross. The ball is in our court. The rest of our lives will only provide a starting place to respond to His love.

Sitting in that parking lot with Keith 11 years later, I thanked God for the precious gift of my husband. But even more so, I thanked God for the gift of His Son. My marriage is a success because my husband and I love Jesus more than we love each other. In order to get a life, we must be sure to snag the right prince. No mortal man can make us happy. Only One can complete us. Only One can quench the desire in our hearts to be loved completely. Only One can guarantee an ending that reads "happily ever after." His name is Jesus.

SPECIALS

Week 3

I'm in a Hurry, So Make It to Go!

Myth #3: A busy life = An Abundant life.

Rapid heart palpitations, sweaty palms, uncontrollable shaking, shortness of breath. Was I coming down with a virus? No, it was much worse. I had misplaced my day planner! In desperation I launched a search party by offering a five dollar reward to the member of my family who could locate the priceless possession. Fortunately, the story has a happy ending. By the end of the day one of my kids was five dollars richer and I had my life back. It's pretty sad that a little black book could throw my life into total disarray.

We live in an on-the-go culture that esteems busyness and constant activity. Where are we going? What are we doing? Does it matter for eternity? Sometimes, in moments of unusual silence, we wonder what God thinks of our pace of life.

This week we will take a look at key factors to running the race called life. The abundant life will be impossible unless we learn to run the race at God's pace. The abundant life cannot be ordered like a fast food item on a to-go menu. Let's take off our running shoes, relax, and dine in. Thanks be to God, we're in for a real treat.

On Your Mark, Get Set, Go!

From the moment we take our first breath, we are off and running in the race called life. In our early years, our race course is defined. For most the message is "run hard, run fast, run to win." Few will ever slow down long enough to question whether they are running on the right course.

Do you know where you are going? Are you on the right course? How tragic that so many will cross the finish line only to discover they were running on the wrong course!

Most of us will find ourselves in one of two races: the rat race or the right race. Those in the rat race will be coached and cheered on by the world, while those in the right race will be coached by God and run for an audience of One. Those in the rat race will run with many, while those in the right race will run with few. Those in the rat race will run for an assortment of worldly and temporal prizes, while those in the right race will run for a lasting, eternal prize. The right race will lead to the abundant life, while the rat race will lead to just a life.

Most of us will find ourselves in one of two races: the rat race or the right race. … The abundant life can only be found by running the right race.

Anyone who has professed a belief in Jesus Christ and acknowledged that He paid the penalty for our sins has qualified for the right race. (see John 3:16; John 14:6) Unfortunately, many Christians have failed to leave the starting block in the right race. The abundant life can only be found by running the right race.

What is the "prize" for the Christian (1 Cor. 9:24-27)?

____

Do you want to run in such a way as to get the prize? (Remember, you do not get the prize by performing works, but rather believing in Jesus. See Ephesians 2:8.) ❑ Yes ❑ No

Which race best represents your life currently: ❑ The right race or ❑ The rat race? If you aren't sure, these questions may help. Rank your responses on the continuums.

1. When making important decisions, my first thought is to:

Consult others ———————————————— Consult God

2. When asked for advice, I am most likely to answer according to:

My own experience ——— Principles set forth in God's Word

3. When meeting someone for the first time, I am most likely to look for ways to:

Make a good first impression ——— Turn the conversation to Christ

4. If I misplaced my Bible, I would:

Not sweat it ——— Notice it missing within 24 hours

5. When setting out to accomplish a big task, I think more about:

Recognition I might receive ——— Glory God might receive

The answers to this self-test speak for themselves. Perhaps your answers indicate you are in the right race. Keep up the good work! For those whose answers indicate they are in the rat race or teetering precariously between the two races, there is still hope. It is never too late to change race courses.

Enter ye in at the strait gate: for wide is the gate, and broad is the way, that leadeth to destruction, and many there be which go in thereat: Because strait is the gate, and narrow is the way, which leadeth unto life, and few there be that find it.
–Matthew 7:13-14, KJV

Read Matthew 7:13-14 in your Bible. Which race does the wide gate and broad road represent? ❑ The right race or ❑ The rat race

Which race does the small gate and narrow road represent?
❑ The right race or ❑ The rat race

Which one leads to "life"? ❑ The right race or ❑ The rat race

How many will find it? ______________________________

Read the same passage in the *King James Version* in the margin. The word *strait* is different from *straight. Straight* means *not crooked; strait* means *pent up, narrow, difficult to be entered.* The road leading to life is difficult. It is not the standard default road or course that most will take without thought or consideration. The narrow, strait road is the unpopular road that only few will choose. Those who choose the narrow road will do so with great effort and thought.

Luke 13:22-27 has always sent a shiver up my spine. Read this passage in your Bible. How does it make you feel?

- ❑ I do not doubt my salvation. I am confident that I have entered through the narrow door.
- ❑ I thought Christianity was like a club. Sign up and you're in.
- ❑ I have reservations about the road I am currently traveling.

What is one truth you would draw from the Scripture you've studied today?

____

____

____

____

My goal today is not to get you to doubt your salvation, but rather to take a fresh and objective look at what the Bible says about the road we travel. Many Christians have confessed with their mouths that Jesus is Lord and believe in their hearts that God raised Him from the dead (see Rom. 10:9) yet have at times chosen the rat race over the right race. I have been one such person.

The goal today is to encourage each of us to take a closer examination of our own lives. If after today you doubt in any way that you are on the right road, let me encourage you to go before God and ask His forgiveness. Express your desire to enter through the narrow gate and commit to the right race.

As you close your study in prayer, review your answers to the self-test on pages 40-41. Ask God to help you in the areas where you need to grow.

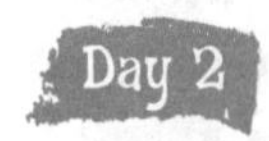

Champions Train to Win

I remember the 1972 Summer Olympics as if it were yesterday. I was only nine years old and my mom had recently signed me up for a gymnastics class. My eyes were glued to the television when Olga Korbut performed her gymnastics routine. Wow! I wanted to be a champion like her! What an inspiration. I believe that moment in 1972 inspired me to pursue gymnastics for the next decade of my life. Over the years, my goals have changed, but my desire to be a champion remains.

Yesterday we addressed the importance of choosing the right race rather than the rat race. For the remainder of the week, we will look at four key factors that distinguish champions from mere contestants. The majority of Christians will run and complete the race as mere contestants; only a few will cross the finish line as champions. I don't know about you, but I'm in the race called life to be a champion. I have yet to meet a true champion in this race who is not experiencing the abundant life that Jesus promised. The abundant life comes as a natural by-product in the life of a champion. Who wouldn't want that?

1. Champions train to win.

Every serious, committed athlete has a passion to win. They don't endure the agony of training for a ribbon that says, "honorable mention." Champions set out to become champions with determination and self-restraint. They hire the very best trainer to assist them in their goal. For the Christian who desires to be a champion, the trainer is God. He designed the race course and created each contestant, so He knows best what it takes to finish as a champion. God has given each Christian everything needed to cross the finish line a champion.

To run with purpose and avoid being a "man running aimlessly" (1 Cor. 9:26), we must have a workout plan. I recall a moment of vanity and ignorance in my college years concerning a workout plan. Spring break was just around the corner and my roommate and I committed to do sit-ups every day to ensure we had washboard abs for our trip to the beach. We stuck to our plan but saw little results. Why? We implemented the plan one week before the trip!

1. Champions train to win.

Can you think of a time when you developed a plan to achieve a goal but failed to initiate it or stay with it long enough? ❑ Yes ❑ No What was it?

____

How did you feel when you failed to accomplish your goal?

____

Champions don't become champions overnight. They commit to a workout plan and discipline themselves to stick to it. What is the workout plan? Fortunately, God has provided Christians with a trainer, the Holy Spirit, and a workout manual, the Bible. An athlete who does not listen to the trainer and follow the trainer's instructions will fail in the pursuit to be a champion. Likewise, a Christian who does not follow the Bible under the direction of the Holy Spirit will not become a champion in the eyes of God. Unfortunately, the race course in the right race is overwhelmed with mere contestants.

The Christians I have met who are champions always have these things in common: They talk to God. They listen to God. They don't budge until they hear from God. They dive into God's Word daily, as if their lives depend on it. To be a champion in the right race, you will have to yield to the Holy Spirit at every juncture.

Direct me in the path
of your commands,
for there I find delight.
–Psalm 119:35

Role: ____________

Your word is a lamp
to my feet
and a light for my path.
–Psalm 119:105

Role: ____________

Your statutes are my
heritage forever;
they are the joy of
my heart.
–Psalm 119:111

Role: ____________

Direct my footsteps accord-
ing to your word;
let no sin rule over me.
–Psalm 119:133

Role: ____________

What is one truth you would draw from the Scripture you've studied today?

____

____

____

Read the verses listed below and write the benefits of trusting God to direct your life.

Scripture	Benefit
Psalm 16:11	____________
Psalm 119:32	____________
Psalm 119:35	____________
Proverbs 3:5-6	____________
Acts 2:28	____________

Champions recognize that God's Word is the compass that guides them in the right race.

Read the verses in the margin and write down the role God's Word plays in directing our course.

Psalm 119 is full of benefits received by obeying God's statutes. This week, commit to read through Psalm 119 and highlight verses that extol the benefits of following God's statutes, commands, and laws.

I love how *The Message* words 1 Corinthians 9:27: "I don't know about you, but I'm running hard for the finish line. I'm giving it everything I've got. No sloppy living for me! I'm staying alert and in top condition. I'm not going to get caught napping, telling everyone else all about it and then missing out myself."

Close today by praying Psalm 25:4-5 from your Bible. The first key factor in becoming a champion is to train to win. Have you enlisted help from the one Trainer who matters in the race called life?

Day 3

Champions Follow Champions

I've heard it said that Christians should live their lives in such a way that others will say, "Take me to your leader." The abundant life is contagious. If we spot someone living it, we want to know how he or she got it. Unfortunately, once we discover it is a life-long pursuit, many of us will give up and settle for running the race as a contestant rather than a champion.

My husband, Keith, is a true champion. He is the kind of person people naturally desire to follow. A couple of years ago, he committed to disciple four men on a weekly basis. What began as a small discipleship group has blossomed into a group of 18 men who meet every Wednesday morning at 6:00 a.m. at a local restaurant. They have grown from a booth to a banquet room.

Keith leads them through a variety of Bible studies that are designed to teach the men how to be godly husbands, fathers, businessmen, etc. Within the group, he matched the men up in pairs so they can meet separately to hold each other accountable in various areas of their Christian lives. One can only begin to imagine the impact the teaching and accountability will have on each man in the group, his friends and coworkers, his family, and the generations to come.

2. Champions follow champions.

Paul was purposeful and intentional about passing the torch of his faith down to Timothy (see 2 Tim. 2:1-2). Champions train champions, who train champions, and so on.

1. Champions train to win.
2. **Champions follow champions.**

Have you been trained or discipled by a champion, and if so, who was it and what impact did such training or discipleship have on your life?

____

____

Are you purposeful about passing the torch of your faith down to others? If you have had the privilege of discipling another person or a group, what did God show you through your experience?

____

____

Let me stop here and commend you for going through this study. It is an indication that you desire to be a champion. When you participate in Bible studies, you are allowing God to speak to you. I enjoy writing Bible studies because women must open their Bibles to find the answers. Heaven knows, God can show you far more than I can!

Not many of you should presume to be teachers, my brothers, because you know that we who teach will be judged more strictly.
–James 3:1

The goal of every champion in training should be to someday train other potential champions. However, we must never take the job of teaching lightly. Read what James 3:1 (in the margin) says regarding those who teach.

For those who serve in matters of the kingdom, our service to Christ should never replace our time with Christ. We never cease to be disciples. In fact, you might be surprised to discover what Christ has to say regarding our service to Him.

Read Luke 10:38-42 in your Bible. Jesus made a point to–
❑ thank Martha for the fabulous hors d'oeuvres and ask for the recipe.
❑ commend Mary for her willingness to sit at His feet.
❑ chastise Mary for leaving Martha the kitchen duty.
❑ gently reprimand Martha for being distracted in serving.

Jesus is not knocking service, but rather making a point that our sitting and listening to Him should always precede our serving. Martha was directly serving Christ, but Jesus made the strong point that " 'only one thing is needed' " and " 'Mary has chosen what is better' " (v. 42). What a statement to those of us who scurry around in Christian service! Mary knew the value of sitting at the feet of Jesus and learning from Him. Everything else could wait. I can just imagine her sitting at His feet hanging on His every word, tuned out to the world around her. If you want to hang on Jesus' every word, you best get in the Word.

If you were to take inventory of a typical day in your life, would it indicate that you prioritize sitting at the feet of Jesus as His disciple? ❑ Yes ❑ No

If no, I challenge you to examine your calendar and commitments and pray about what you can change or take off your plate to make time for the one thing that is needed. Write your thoughts in the margin.

Several years ago, God convicted me to prioritize sitting at the feet of Jesus as His disciple. I had to evaluate what could be removed from my plate and take action. I scaled back on the number of speaking engagements I do each year, hired needed staff to help with ministry duties, and most importantly, finally learned to say no!

Are you more like Mary or Martha? ______________________________

My dear Martha friends, as a fellow Martha and a Mary wanna-be, I feel your pain. My turning point came several years ago, when I realized that my motives in serving Jesus were not entirely pure. God began to show me that my inability to say no was directly related to my desire to please others, and an erroneous belief that I needed to serve God to please Him. We live in a world that esteems performance.

Nothing will rob a woman of the abundant life quicker than a schedule so packed that it leaves little time to sit at the feet of Jesus. Don't misunderstand me. I am not saying to avoid serving. Nor am I citing Luke 10:38-42 as an excuse to sit and never serve. The key is balance. The natural by-product of sitting at the feet of Jesus should be the desire to serve Him.

As part of my commitment to prioritize sitting at the feet of Jesus over merely serving Jesus, I made a personal vow to read through the Bible every year for the rest of my life. No small goal, but as a ministry leader I feel I have no right speaking and writing about God's truths unless I am in God's Word daily.

I am hyper to the core and sitting still does not come naturally for me. If I can learn to sit at the feet of Jesus daily, so can you. If we want to be champions, we must take the time to learn from the ultimate Champion, Jesus.

What is one truth you would draw from the Scripture you've studied today?

____

____

____

____

On a separate sheet of paper or in your prayer journal, take the changes you listed in the margin on page 46 and write a plan to help you spend more time sitting at the feet of Jesus. Ask someone to hold you accountable in the weeks to come.

As you close today, ask God to help you follow the one true Champion in the race called life.

Day 4

Champions Avoid Burnout

I remember a Christian speaker I heard at a women's function years ago. God had obviously gifted her, and her message inspired many of the women in attendance. She was a champion in training. However, I was disappointed to hear that several years later she had an affair with a married man in her church, divorced her husband, dropped out of ministry, and last I heard was not even attending church.

We can all probably think of someone who was a champion-in-the-making, and, for whatever reasons, dropped out of the race. Many well-meaning Christians will dive into serving Christ and years later crash and burn. How does this happen? Among many reasons, burnout can be a chief cause. When Christians fail to safeguard against it, they will usually suffer the consequences.

Today we look at the third key factor in the pursuit to become a champion in the race called life.

1. Champions train to win.
2. Champions follow champions.
3. **Champions avoid burnout.**

3. Champions avoid burnout.

Even marathon runners need to refuel along the way. Why do Christians think they can go full speed and not suffer serious consequences when they fail to refuel?

Your busiest day in ministry would not begin to compare to any day out of the public ministry of Jesus. He was given the awesome responsibility of teaching and paying for a new covenant between God and His people. Jesus' job meant founding a new world religion. He had the daunting task of equipping others to spread the wonderful news of God's forgiveness and unconditional love. And He only had three years to do it! Jesus was fully human, so He must have felt overwhelmed at times. Every moment of every day was critical in His three-year public ministry, and somehow He managed without a day planner or a Palm Pilot!

Let's take a look at an average day in the life of Jesus. Read Matthew 14:13-21. Where was Jesus going and for what purpose (v. 13)?

____

How did Jesus respond to the crowd (v. 14)?

____

Jesus' impromptu healing session lasted well into the late afternoon. Rather than send the people away as the disciples suggested, He went on to feed over 5000 people with 5 loaves of bread and 2 fish. He never glanced down at His watch or checked His calendar to see if He had a conflict.

After feeding the 5000, what did Jesus do next (Matt. 14:23)?

____

After a long and strenuous day healing people, preaching, and feeding 5000, Jesus retreated to a mountainside to be alone and pray. Sometime later that evening He joined His disciples back on the boat. Once the boat landed in Gennesaret, people recognized Jesus and word quickly spread to the surrounding country (see Matt. 14:34-36).

Once again, people brought the sick to Jesus for healing. Many begged Him to let their sick family and friends touch the edge of His cloak. All who touched Him were healed. As busy as Jesus was, He had the fuel He needed to face another busy day.

What did He do to "refuel"? ______________________________

He recognized the absolute necessity of spending time with His Heavenly Father. How about you? Do you make it a habit to spend time alone with God? ❑ Yes ❑ No

List the activities Jesus accomplished in the day recorded in Mark 1:21-34.

____

After teaching in the synagogue, casting out a demon, and healing Simon's mother-in-law, His day was still not over. The town gathered at His door and He healed the sick and demon-possessed. Talk about putting in a hard day at the office! I bet He slept well that night.

Read Mark 1:35 and check the correct answer. The next morning, Jesus–

❑ hit the snooze bar several times when His alarm went off.
❑ got up and sought out a solitary place to pray.
❑ called in sick. After all He did the day before, who would blame Him?
❑ grabbed the paper and headed out for a double latte.

Jesus modeled the importance of taking time to pray in the midst of busy days.

Do you currently have a set time each day where you spend time alone in prayer? ❑ Yes ❑ No If not, what hinders you from doing so?

____

Take inventory of an average day. When can you set aside time for prayer if you are not doing so already?

____

If our days are too busy to allow for prayer, our days are too busy. We must change our schedules to allow for time with God each day. This is especially true if we serve in ministry-related endeavors. Those who fail to prioritize prayer will lack the energy needed to finish the race a champion. Those who meet with God, the Trainer, on a daily basis will logically look to Him for direction. Prayer is a critical factor in running the race at God's pace.

What is one truth you would draw from the Scripture you've studied today?

____

____

____

____

Close today by asking God to help you prioritize daily prayer, if you are not doing so already. If prayer is already a priority for you, pray for the rest of us!

Champions Focus on the Finish Line

OK, I confess, I'm a hopeless over-achiever. I even had to have my mid-life crisis early. It happened when I hit my 30s. Fortunately, I didn't go as far as to trade in my minivan for a convertible or schedule an appointment for Botox injections. I did, however, begin to question many of the things in my life and ask myself, "Does what I do matter for eternity? What sort of legacy am I leaving my children? Am I fulfilling God's purpose for my life?" The milestones formed by certain birthdays make the threshold of eternity seem a bit closer.

What was I aiming for in the race called life? Prizes? Fame? Success? Did it have eternal value and significance? Through this painful self-analysis, I came to a worthy conclusion: Champions focus on the finish line. They run the race with an eternal perspective. They run for a prize that has lasting value. They live for the day they will cross the finish line a champion.

Today we will discuss the fourth key factor in the pursuit to be a champion.

1. Champions train to win.
2. Champions follow champions.
3. Champions avoid burnout.
4. **Champions focus on the finish line.**

4. Champions focus on the finish line.

In the margin, list some of the prizes you have been awarded in past years in which you have taken great pride. (service awards, accomplishments, etc.)

Read Philippians 3:7-14. Write the word *Rubbish* over your list. Do you count your earthly prizes as loss for the sake of Christ?

What will happen to our work according to 1 Corinthians 3:10-15?

____

How humbling! All the time, effort, blood, sweat, and tears and poof, it may be incinerated. Many Christians are running for prizes that will someday turn to dust. How unfortunate that we sometimes falsely link the gathering of earthly prizes to experiencing the abundant life. I must admit to a time in my life when I did so. During my time of self-analysis (otherwise known as "mid-life crisis"), I realized that much of what I had chosen to invest my time in was of temporary significance.

The biggest challenge comes in Philippians 3:10: "I want to know Christ and the power of his resurrection and the fellowship of sharing in his sufferings, becoming like him in his death." Do you want to know Christ? I'm sure you answered yes, but let me ask you this: are you willing to share in His sufferings and become like Him in His death?

You may be hesitant to answer because you don't know what you are signing up for. Have you ever wept over a particular sin? Not because of discipline or consequences that may occur as a result of it, but because Jesus had to suffer and die because of it?

"Do not store up for yourselves treasures on earth, where moth and rust destroy, and where thieves break in and steal. But store up for yourselves treasures in heaven, where moth and rust do not destroy, and where thieves do not break in and steal. For where your treasure is, there your heart will be also."
–Matthew 6:19-21

Write your own paraphrase of Hebrews 12:2 below.

____

____

Who set the race before us? ____________________________

How do we run the race with endurance? ____________________

Whom does our faith depend on from start to finish? _____________

For the Christian, the finish line is really the start line! Our brief stay on this earth is just a dot on the timeline of eternity. The problem is that most Christians are short-sighted and live for the dot rather than the line. Our time here on earth is just a training mission for eternity. We must make the finish line the single object in our view. But what's beyond the finish line? Heaven!

When you think of heaven, what comes to mind?

- ❑ I know it's home, but I'm not homesick yet!
- ❑ I look forward to being reunited with loved ones who have gone before me.
- ❑ Mansion, sports court, swimming pool, and no kitchen duty.
- ❑ Better brush up on the hymns.
- ❑ Only one thing: Jesus!

Do you look forward to heaven? It's hard to imagine what heaven is like when this life is all we know. In my early years as a Christian, I wasn't too keen on heaven. Would I be bored? Would I have to live by myself in my big mansion? Would I have my family? Would there be a Starbucks? I could not picture what heaven would look like. When I tried, it came out looking like endless choir rehearsals with singing, singing, and more singing. Unfortunately, I can't carry a tune, so I pictured myself relegated to the back of the risers in the tone-deaf section.

Now it's your turn. How do you picture heaven? Draw a picture or write your description below.

Read Philippians 1:21 in the margin. Explain what this verse means to you.

To me, to live is Christ and to die is gain.
–Philippians 1:21

____

____

The longer I run in the race called life, the closer I grow to my Trainer. The closer I am to my Trainer, the more I long to meet Him face-to-face. Heaven does not seem as daunting when you view it as a homecoming. Can you honestly say that you view crossing the finish line as gain?

Dick Hoyt and his son, Rick, entered the Ironman Triathlon World Championships in Hawaii in 1999. In this particular race, competitors have to swim 2.4 miles through the ocean and then peddle a bicycle 112 miles before running a hilly, 26.2 mile marathon. It would take Dick Hoyt and his son, Rick, 16 hours and 14 minutes to finish the 140 mile day of reckoning. They wouldn't finish at the front, but their goal was to simply finish.

Why did this father/son team make the news everywhere? They were the first tandem to ever complete the Ironman Triathlon World Championships together. What made their story newsworthy is that Dick's son, Rick, is handicapped. In the triathlon swim, Rick laid on his back in a rubber raft attached by rope to a wet suit vest worn by his father, as his father swam 2.4 miles. In the bike portion of the race, Rick sat in a chair attached to the front of his father's bike, as his father peddled 112 miles. In the running portion of the race, Rick's dad pushed him in a race chair for the final 26.2 miles to the finish. Without his father, Rick could not have finished the race.

We, too, are handicapped in the race called life. To run the race with endurance, we must depend on our Father every step of the way. The Greek word for *race* is *agon*, which is where we get the word, *agony*. God never said the race would be an easy jog. The Christian race is a demanding and sometimes grueling long distance run. However, God desires to run in tandem with us every step of the way. When we are weary or tempted to quit, He is willing to pick us up and carry us, if need be.

On the day I cross the finish line, I want to run into the loving arms of my Savior and pick right up where we left off. Truly, the world's finish line is the Christian's start line. I don't know about you, but I'm in this race to be a champion. Like Paul, I want to say, "I have fought the good fight, I have finished the race, I have kept the faith" (2 Tim. 4:7). Should I be awarded a prize on that day, it will be an honor and a privilege to cast it at the feet of my Savior. The victory is in Jesus.

What is one truth you would draw from the Scripture you've studied today?

____

____

____

____

Truth to Go

As I mentioned in the introduction to this week's study, our culture esteems busyness and constant activity. Do the things you spend your time on matter for eternity? Is your motive for saying yes related to your desire to please others or to a belief that you need to serve God to please Him?

Nothing will rob you of the abundant life quicker than a schedule that is so packed it leaves little time to sit at the feet of Jesus. The answer isn't to avoid serving. The answer is balance. That's what the Lord desires for us. That's an abundant life.

Week 4

I'll Have What She's Having, Please

Myth #4: Material possessions will lead to peace and purpose.

If you could be anyone in the world, who would you want to be? Sadly, few women would answer, "me." Are you satisfied with who you are? Are you satisfied with your house, your husband, your lack of a husband, your children, your lack of children, your job, your life? How about this one: Are you satisfied with your body shape? Gotcha! Even the most satisfied woman would be tempted to change something if a genie appeared and offered to grant her three wishes.

Hold your hand in front of your mouth. If you can feel breath coming out, you have most likely compared yourself to another person. It is human nature. I have done it in the past and still struggle with it at times. There was a time in my life when, even though I knew Truth, I falsely imagined having an abundant life was contingent on such things as my husband's salary, my children's behavior, and whether or not I could wear a size 2. (I can't, so hold off on the hate mail.) And that's only an abbreviated version of my comparison list.

Wanting something you do not have is not evil in and of itself. However, if a person becomes too focused on satisfying their wants, it is certain to prevent the abundant life. How ironic! The very quest for what the world promises will lead to a better life really only leads to emptiness and despair.

Before you order what someone else is having, you may want to think twice. You might be surprised to discover the Chef's Special has been in front of you all along.

If Only I Had Her Paycheck, Personality, Body, and Beau!

I hate shopping for blue jeans. I recently spent an entire day trying to find a pair of blue jeans to compliment my figure. Now there's an oxymoron: jeans and compliment. I was amazed at how much bigger they look on the hanger. How depressing to have to lie down on the dressing room floor just to get them buttoned. If breathing wasn't important to me, I would have bought them. I finally settled on a pair of Levis. I love how they don't have sizes but rather waist and length measurements. They figured out how to market to a woman's desire to be in denial when it comes to her pant size. Not that it helped in my case. I ended up with the same waist and length measurement. Yippee. It's official. I'm shaped like a square.

Years ago a day like that would have left me asking, "Why can't I have a figure like _____?" Comparing yourself to others can quickly spread to other areas of your life as well. Before you know it you are comparing your husband to others, your children to others, your house to others, until you reduce yourself to a quivering lump!

Now it's your turn. Take an honest and introspective look at yourself. What areas of your life, if changed, would enable you to have a more abundant life? Stop and pray. Ask God to help you be honest with yourself as we look at true contentment.

Read the statements below but don't actually fill in the blanks.

I would be happier if …
I could have the job of ___________ and the income of ___________.
My husband was more like _____ and my children were more like _____.
I looked like ___________ and had a personality like ___________.
I could wear a size ___________ and weigh ___________ pounds.

As you read through the statements above, answers may have quickly come to mind. Or perhaps you found that you are more content with your life than you realized.

When it comes to our looks, shape, or basic personality, the core of who we are cannot be changed. We can do things to accentuate our basic inborn features, but we cannot change them altogether.

I praise you because I am fearfully and wonderfully made; your works are wonderful, I know that full well
–Psalm 139:14

Read Psalm 139:14 out loud. Now, consider how it would read if you fill in the blanks below.

I praise you because I am fearfully and wonderfully made; your works are wonderful, I know that full well. However, I would prefer to look more like __________, have a body like __________, and a personality like __________.

Wouldn't that sound absurd? Don't slight God on His creation. You are fearfully and wonderfully made. Do you know that full well?

If you are married, you have probably compared your husband to another man. Even single women struggle at times with a desire for someone else's spouse. We can learn from David as he struggled with temptation regarding another man's spouse (see 2 Sam. 11:2-5). David *saw* Bathsheba, he *desired* Bathsheba, and then he *acted* upon his desires.

List the three words in italics above, in order:

__________________ __________________ __________________

Place an X on the line where you think sin began for David.

Once David acted on his desire, what followed was a web of lies and deceit that left one man murdered; a child dead; and David guilt-ridden, broken, and grief-stricken. But it all started with desire.

We see a man who appears to have it all together. If we allow our minds to progress from seeing to desiring, acting upon the desire is only one step away. If you find yourself wondering, "What might it be like to be married to ____?" stop and pray. Ask God to quench any desire you have for another man, ask for His forgiveness, and immediately begin to thank Him for qualities you admire in your husband. If you are single, thank Him for the fact that you are betrothed to the one perfect Man!

Matthew 5:27-28 explains that it is possible to commit adultery with someone in our hearts. WARNING: If you experience an ongoing struggle of desire

Command those who are rich in this present world not to be arrogant nor to put their hope in wealth, which is so uncertain, but to put their hope in God, who richly provides us with everything for our enjoyment. Command them to do good, to be rich in good deeds, and to be generous and willing to share. In this way they will lay up treasure for themselves as a firm foundation for the coming age, so that they may take hold of the life that is truly life.
–1 Timothy 6:17-19

for another man, seek out someone you can confess this to and ask her to hold you accountable on a regular basis. I have seen many marriages that could have been saved had things only been nipped in the bud at the desire stage.

Years ago a friend of mine confided that she found herself thinking often of a man other than her husband. I asked her these key questions: "What would you do if you found yourself alone with this man and he shared that the desire was mutual? How would you respond? Would you flee temptation or stick around to see what happened?" She answered very honestly, and I encouraged her to find immediate accountability. She did and today her marriage is intact.

OK. I don't like such direct confrontation either. Let's change the topic to money. When it comes to financial stability we probably all wonder at times if life would be easier if we were rolling in the dough. I've heard it said, "Money won't buy happiness, but it sure helps." According to Scripture, money is not only a deterrent to the abundant life, but it can prevent it altogether.

Look up these verses and list the disadvantages to wealth and riches.

Scripture	Disadvantages of wealth and riches
Psalm 49:16-20	______________________
Proverbs 23:4-5	______________________
Ecclesiastes 5:10	______________________
Ecclesiastes 5:12	______________________
Matthew 19:23-24	______________________
1 Timothy 6:9-10	______________________

What is one truth you would draw from the Scripture you've studied today?

____

____

____

____

My husband and I have friends who benefited significantly when a high tech company the husband founded grew rapidly and went public on the stock market. Their net worth skyrocketed overnight. The husband said God had gifted him with making money so he could give it away.

He and his wife gave millions of dollars away to our local church and a variety of Christian causes. What I love most about this couple is that they are extremely humble and down to earth. They acknowledge that God has entrusted the money to them to further His work here on earth. They are generous, willing to share, and thus, have taken hold of "the life that is truly life" (1 Tim. 6:19). Our friends are experiencing the abundant life not because of their wealth, but in spite of it.

As you close today, ask God to make you aware of areas in which you struggle with discontentment. Ask Him to satisfy you according to His truths.

No Fair!

When I was a child, my younger brother and I counted our gifts under the Christmas tree to make sure we had the same number. As we got older, we would actually calculate the total dollar value of all our gifts after unwrapping them. If it didn't seem to even up, the jilted party screamed, "No fair!" Now, as a parent of three children who have resorted to counting their gifts under the tree, I have apologized to my parents.

We can all think of times in our lives when things haven't seemed to even up and we've been left crying, "No fair!" Every one of us can probably remember getting a "life isn't always fair" pep talk from our parents. What does God have to say about fairness and equality? He addresses it in Matthew 20:1-16.

The Jews divided their days into 12 equal parts, or hours, beginning at sunrise and ending at sunset. The working day began at 6:00 a.m. and ended at 6:00 p.m. Scripture says the landowner went out to find workers to work in his vineyard. It looked something like this:

6:00 a.m.: (work day begins) Landowner hired first batch of workers.
9:00 a.m.: Landowner hired next batch of workers.
12:00 p.m.: Landowner hired more workers.
3:00 p.m.: Landowner hired more workers.
5:00 p.m.: Landowner hired last batch of workers.
6:00 p.m.: (work day ends) Foreman called workers in to receive pay.

How much did the landowner tell the first group of workers he would pay them? ______________________________

How much did the landowner tell the second group of workers he would

pay them? ____

How much did the landowner pay each group of workers? ___________

The landowner told the first group outright that he would pay them each a denarius. He told the remaining groups that he would pay them "whatever is right."

Do you think his decision to pay the latter groups the same pay as the first group was right? ❑ Yes ❑ No ❑ Not Sure

The first group of workers worked 12 full hours and got 1 denarius. The last group of workers worked 1 hour and got 1 denarius.

What did the first group of workers complain about?

____

Did the landowner fulfill his end of the agreement to the first group of workers? ❑ Yes ❑ No How did the landowner respond to their complaints?

____

Do you agree with the landowner's defense? ❑ Yes ❑ No

Can you think of a situation where you felt that God blessed someone more than you? ❑ Yes ❑ No Explain.

____

____

The truth is, God has the right to bless whoever He wants, whenever He wants. God is sovereign and the ultimate owner of all we have (see 1 Chron. 29:11-12). He is entitled to do what He wills with what He owns in the first place. It may not make sense to us at the time, or for that matter, ever. However, we can be assured that God works all things together for good for those who love and follow Him (see Rom. 8:28).

How does the truth that God can bless or not bless as He pleases make you feel?

❏ Great, as long as I'm on the receiving end.
❏ Who does He think He is?
❏ Father knows best.
❏ I'm not sure.

God imparts the same truth in the story of the prodigal son. The younger son asked for his inheritance up front. His father granted his request. The son then left home and squandered his money on wild living. He found himself in a job feeding pigs and longing for the pods the pigs were eating. Finally it occurred to him that his father's hired workers had more than he had. He decided to return home and beg his father to hire him as a worker. Then the father threw a party honoring the son's return.

What was the older son's complaint according to Luke 15:25-32?

____

____

Can you think of a time when you did the right thing and someone you believed to be less deserving got the reward? ❏ Yes ❏ No
If yes, explain.

____

We do not have the capacity to fully know why God blesses some and not others. But God is not out to get us. He is loving and certainly no stranger to injustice Himself. When God watched His sinless and perfect Son die on a cross for sinful mankind we didn't hear Him crying, "No fair." In fact, it was His idea. No doubt, we were on the receiving end with that blessing.

The concept of grace is even more amazing. Unlike the group of workers who only worked 1 hour and received the same pay as those who worked 12 hours, we fare far better than they did. We did nothing to deserve the incredible blessing of forgiveness that God has given us. That is the definition of grace.

Close today by thanking God for the many blessings you have received. Thank Him for offering forgiveness in place of your sinfulness with the death of His Son. Thank God that, as Christians, we didn't get what our actions deserved.

What is one truth you would draw from the Scripture you've studied today?

____

____

____

____

The World Says I Can Have it All ... But Do I Really Want it?

Be self-controlled and alert. Your enemy the devil prowls around like a roaring lion looking for someone to devour. Resist him, standing firm in the faith, because you know that your brothers throughout the world are undergoing the same kind of sufferings.
–1 Peter 5:8-9

If you harbor bitter envy and selfish ambition in your hearts, do not boast about it or deny the truth. Such "wisdom" does not come down from heaven but is earthly, unspiritual, of the devil. For where you have envy and selfish ambition, there you find disorder and every evil practice.
–James 3:14-16

I have met women who are absolutely miserable because their husbands or children are failing to meet their expectations. I have met women whose happiness ebbs and flows, depending on the read-out on their scales. I have met women who are so obsessed with getting a bigger house that their current house ceases to be a home.

I have also met women who are in unhappy marriages but are experiencing the abundant life. I have met women who have children who have broken their hearts, yet they are filled with joy in Christ. I have met women who have struggled most of their lives with their weight, yet their lives are testimonies to the power of God. I have met women who live in small, modest homes, but they are experiencing the abundant life. Nothing is wrong with hoping and praying for improvement in areas of our lives, but danger comes when our happiness depends on it.

What is the secret to the abundant life for the people I mentioned? They are more obsessed with God than the current item on their wish lists. The world has fooled us into thinking that we can have it all. It offers a quick-fix solution for every problem. Don't like your husband? Swap him out for another one. Not happy with your weight? Take a pill or try the new fad diet. We're so busy spinning our wheels that we've failed to see who's behind the whole plot. Satan! He's crafty and he knows that if he can get people to believe they can have it all, they won't have time for the one thing that really matters: God!

What words does Peter use to describe Satan in 1 Peter 5:8-9?

____

How should we prepare for his schemes?

____

____

What is the origin of envy and selfish ambition according to James 3:14-16?

____

Read the following verses and fill in the blanks:

"A heart at peace gives ________________ to the body,

but envy ________________ the bones" (Prov. 14:30).

"I saw that all labor and all achievement spring from man's envy of his

________________. This too is ________________, a chasing after the wind" (Eccl. 4:4).

Recently, my 11-year-old daughter and I experienced a standoff on an outing to the mall. (All you moms with daughters who have left the nest, this is your cue to snicker and breathe a huge sigh of relief.) The stimulus to this standoff was my daughter's request for a new backpack. Oddly enough, I had just purchased a new backpack for her a couple of months prior. She had picked it out herself and said something to the effect of, "I love it! It's to die for!" Now, she informed me, she wanted a different one. You know, one like Annie Greiner's. I said no, reminded her that she had a perfectly good backpack, and further reminded her that we don't always get everything we want and should appreciate what we have. I was strong. I was firm. I was mother-of-the-hour.

Several weeks later I was shopping without my daughter and that backpack was on the clearance rack for $6.99! I could just picture her face, lighting up with joy upon receiving it! At a price like that, how could I refuse? I stood there for what seemed like hours, and then finally walked away.

We live in a culture where most people get what they want and want for very little. If we grow tired of something, we replace it. God has shown me personally how dangerous this mindset can be, especially if we pass it down to our children. Children who are not accustomed to hearing, "no" or "wait" when they ask for something will struggle with self-restraint in their adult years. What if they marry and grow weary of their spouse? Divorce! What if their house is never big enough? Move! What if they can't afford to take nice vacations like the Joneses? Charge it!

If our children do not learn to accept "no" or "wait" when they are young, they will struggle to accept "no" or "wait" from God. Satan cheers when Christians get focused on wanting what they do not have. He knows they will have little impact on the kingdom if they are busy running for the world's prizes.

Jesus is certainly no stranger to Satan's schemes. Satan attempted to snow Him with the same lie he tells us today: "You can have it all!"

Fill in the following chart based on Luke 4:1-13.

Satan's offer to Jesus	Jesus' response to Satan
1. ______________________	______________________
2. ______________________	______________________
3. ______________________	______________________

Laying aside all malice, all deceit, hypocrisy, envy, and all evil speaking, as newborn babes, desire the pure milk of the word, that you may grow thereby, if indeed you have tasted that the Lord is gracious.
–1 Peter 2:1-3, NKJV

Jesus was able to withstand the temptation because He knew the Word of God! Reread Luke 4:9-11. Who else knew the Word of God?

____

Satan is wise, crafty, and single-minded. He wants you and me missing the abundant life, but he doesn't stop there. He knows if we want what we do not have, we will assuredly pass that fixation down for generations to come until someone has the guts to break the chain and say, "Enough!" If you have been trained to believe this lie, will you be the one to break the chain?

According to 1 Peter 2:1-3, how do we rid ourselves of envy?

____

What is one truth you would draw from the Scripture you've studied today?

____

____

____

____

The Greek word for *desire* is *epipotheo* (ep-ee-poth-eh'-o), which means *to yearn or intensely crave.* Do you intensely crave the pure milk of the Word? I hope so, because the only defense against envy is to know and live God's Word. If you do not crave the pure milk of God's Word, perhaps you have forgotten the taste of the Lord's graciousness upon your life. Once you've tasted it, you won't order anything else.

Close today by asking God to replace any yearning you may have for the things of the world with an intense craving for the pure milk of His Word. The abundant life depends on it. The only way to have it all is to look to God for His provision.

Is the Grass Always Greener on the Other Side?

Have you ever wanted something so badly that you hesitated to ask God for fear He'd say no? The summer before my daughter entered second grade, many of my friends with second graders requested a teacher who was rumored to be the best. I followed suit. Only the best for my little girl. One week before school started, I received the class list in the mail. She didn't get the teacher I requested!

After a few days of sulking, I realized I never asked for God's will. I did pray that my daughter would get the teacher I requested. I didn't want to ruin her chances by praying and asking God for His will! God's will ultimately prevailed, regardless of the fact that I had not solicited it. That year was one of my daughter's best years ever. Her teacher was a perfect match for my daughter. It's been five years now and my daughter still talks about Mrs. Thomas. Praise God I didn't get my way!

What did the elders of Israel request of Samuel (1 Sam. 8:4-8)?

____

Why? ____

Can you believe it? Grown adults whining for a king so they could be just like everyone else! Stop and think about it for a minute. God was their king at the time they requested a king! Who in the world could Samuel possibly appoint that could manage the people better than God? I wonder if it ever crossed their minds that the problem was not with God's system, but rather their refusal to follow Him.

What did God through Samuel warn the people that a king would do (1 Sam. 8:9-18)?

Verse 11: ___________________________________

Verse 12: ___________________________________

Verse 13: ______________________________

Verse 14: ______________________________

Verse 15: ______________________________

Verse 16: ______________________________

Verse 17: ______________________________

Verse 18: ______________________________

How did the Israelites respond in 1 Samuel 8:19-22?
❑ They came to their senses and begged God for forgiveness.
❑ Waaaaagh. Waaaaagh. We want to be just like the other nations!
❑ Sorry, God, but just trust us on this one. We know what we're doing.

God granted Israel's wish to have a king. The period of the kings, documented in 1 Kings and 2 Kings lasted over 400 years, and an overwhelming majority of the kings who ruled in Israel and Judah did evil in the eyes of the Lord. Everything the prophet Samuel warned the people of transpired. I wonder if Israel would make the same choice again.

Was there a time when you really wanted something because everyone else had it, yet you knew it was not in God's will? ❑ Yes ❑ No
If yes, what were the circumstances?

____

____

Did you pursue it anyway? ❑ Yes ❑ No

How did you feel afterwards?
❑ Angry! I didn't get it.
❑ Praise God, I didn't get my desire!
❑ Great! I would do it again.
❑ Somewhat empty. It didn't quite satisfy.

Psalm 106:6-12 is a brief summary of the Israelite's rebellion in the wilderness before God led them into the promised land. They had witnessed the 10 plagues and been spared, were delivered out of Egypt, witnessed the parting of the Red

Sea, were led by a cloud by day and a pillar of fire by night, observed Moses turn bitter water to sweet water, ate manna that rained down from heaven, saw Moses bring water from a rock, and defeated their opponents with the help of God.

Write Psalm 106:12 in the space below.

____

____

My paraphrase of Exodus 16:1-4 reads, "Waaaaaaagh. We're hungry! We want to go back to Egypt where we were slaves. Remember Egypt? The place we begged You to deliver us from?"

How long had it been since they left Egypt (v. 1)? ________________

It had been approximately six weeks since they were delivered from Egypt! Did they not think that the same God who performed the miracles of the 10 plagues and the parting of the Red Sea was capable of feeding them?

Read Exodus 16:6-8 to find out how God responded to their hunger pangs. What did Moses tell the people God would do?

____

In verses 7 and 8, what did Moses tell the people God had heard?

____

He heard their grumbling! Regardless, He rained manna down from heaven to satisfy their hunger. However, the Israelite's awe and wonder over the miracle quickly wore off and they began to whine for meat.

What do the Israelites claim to miss from Egypt in Numbers 11:4-6?

____

Review Exodus 1:8-14. How were the Israelites treated in Egypt?

____

Then they believed
His words;
They sang His praise.
They soon forgot
His works;
They did not wait for
His counsel,
But lusted exceedingly
in the wilderness,
And tested God in
the desert.
And He gave them
their request,
But sent leanness
into their soul.
–Psalm 106:12-15, NKJV

How did God respond to the Israelite's oppression in Exodus 3:7-9?

❑ He ignored them. Bitter labor builds character.

❑ He empathized with their plight with great compassion and pledged to rescue them.

❑ He called them whiners and told them to get back to work.

What is one truth you would draw from the Scripture you've studied today?

____

____

____

____

Sounds like the Israelites are experiencing a sudden memory loss. It appears that they didn't leave Egypt kicking and screaming, clinging to their pots of meat and precious cucumbers and leeks.

Have you ever prayed for something, God granted your request, and later you grumbled about it? ❑ Yes ❑ No If so, describe the circumstances?

____

____

End today by meditating on the passage in the margin. Let us always be sure that when we ask something of God, it is in His will. If He grants our request, let us express gratitude rather than grumble and complain.

Day 5

The Secret to Contentment: An Attitude of Gratitude

An old Civil War story tells of an Illinois farmer discovered kneeling at the head of a soldier's grave in Nashville. Asked, " 'Is that your boy?' he replied, 'No: he lived in our town, and I have come to find his grave.' The observer said, 'Perhaps you represent his father, who could not come?'–'Yes, my neighbor was glad to have me come; but I came for myself.' "

He went on to explain, " 'You see I had seven children, all of them small; and my wife was sickly. I was drafted. There was nobody to carry on the farm; and I could not hire a substitute. My thirteen dollars a month would not feed the family. It seemed as though I must go, and they must suffer. When we were in our greatest trouble about it,–just the morning I was to report at camp,–my neighbor's son came over to the house, and offered to go to war for me. He said, he had nobody depending on him, and could go better than I. He went, and was wounded at Chickamauga; was brought to a Nashville hospital; and this is his grave.' The farmer had come a long distance, at heavy cost, to write upon the headboard of his soldier friend, 'Died for me.' "[1]

Can you imagine that kind of sacrifice? If you are a Christian, of course you can! We have each been drafted into a battle against sin and death. We will not win unless Someone who has overcome sin and death agrees to take our place on the battlefield. Ladies, the cross represents the headstone of the One who took our place. Stop and picture yourself kneeling before the cross of Calvary. It is rugged, worn, and stained with blood. If you could write a note on it, what would it be?

The cross isn't big enough to contain my words. The root of gratitude is the cross. The world esteems positive thinking, but positive thinking comes from positively knowing that we deserve nothing but death. Can you say that out loud? "I deserve death." When the Truth behind the cross takes root in your heart, you will see the world in a new light. You will be grateful for every breath you take because it means you are living. You will be grateful for your imperfect spouse because you have met the One who is perfect. You will be grateful for your children who sometimes disobey because they are gifts on loan from God. You will be grateful with what you have because of what you have been given.

How many lepers did Jesus heal according to Luke 17:11-19? ____________

How many returned to thank Him? ____________________

How did the man express his gratitude? ____________________

____

Why do you think the other nine men failed to show gratitude to Jesus for healing them?

____

____

____

____

Many people go through life thinking the world owes them something. To take blessings for granted is easy. One of the keys to contentment is being grateful for what we have rather than focusing on what we think we should have.

Recently, my family spent the holidays at my in-law's ranch in East Texas. When returning from an outing with the entire family piled into two SUVs, the kids made it a contest to see which car would get home first (without speeding, of course). As we pulled onto the road leading to the house behind the other car, the kids let out a groan. Then from the back seat, my five year-old nephew, Cooper, said, "At least we came in second." What an optimist!

I am an extremely optimistic person, but it has not always been that way. Shortly after my third child, Hayden, was born, I found myself getting more and more negative. I complained about everything. Ryan, my oldest child, had started kindergarten and pick-up time was right smack in the middle of the baby's nap, so I had to wake him up every day to go get his brother. My middle child didn't know the meaning of the word nap and needed constant attention. The house was in a constant state of disarray.

One morning at Bible study my leader, who has two grown boys, shared how she missed seeing the toys in the floor, going to ball games, and even driving carpool! Her house was very clean and quiet, yet she missed them. That was a defining moment in my life. I did not want to look back and regret that I had not made the most of every moment God gave me with my family. Slowly I began to make a concentrated effort to see the positive side of everything. I turned my grumbling to singing and made the kids sing with me. Today, seven years later, not a day goes by that I don't thank God out loud for something. More importantly, I thank God out loud to my children, so I can model an attitude of gratitude.

What is one truth you would draw from the Scripture you've studied today?

____

____

____

____

Think back to our discussion of the Israelites and their sudden memory loss of all they had seen God do. They began to focus on what they did not have, rather than what they had already been given. What is the caution given in Deuteronomy 4:9-10; Deuteronomy 6:10-12; and Hosea 13:6?

____

____

____

Truth to Go

We must never forget the wonderful things God has done. He is the author of every blessing we receive, every breath we take, and the very author of life itself. Contentment requires us to be grateful for what we have rather than to be focused on what we think we should have. We must cultivate the habit of expressing our gratefulness to God each and every day.

Regardless of circumstances in life, the Christian is without excuse when it comes to having an attitude of gratitude. Just like the man who paid tribute to the neighbor boy who fought and died in his place, we, too, stand free from death in the shadow of the cross. Etched on the beautiful cross is the epitaph, "He died for me." That truth alone is reason enough to be grateful for the remainder of our days. If we have God's provision, we truly do have it all!

---

[1]Elon Foster, *6000 Sermon Illustrations: An Omnibus of Classic Sermon Illustrations* (Grand Rapids: Baker Book House, 1952), 317–18.

Menu
1
2
3
4

Week 5

I'll Take the #1 with Extra Me-O

Myth #5: It's all about me.

From the time the first set of rules was issued in the garden of Eden, man has sought a way to break them. God said, "Let's do it this way." Man said, "Let's do it my way." The battle of the wills between God and man has continued ever since. We are born innately self-focused and selfish. If you don't believe me, place a toy in the middle of a group of toddlers and observe what transpires. "Mine" is on the top-10 list of words in every toddler's vocabulary. As they get older, "mine" translates into, "It's all about me."

Even our quest for happiness and the abundant life is self-focused. We seek to satisfy the desires of our hearts. We often pray more for ourselves than for others. Many times we are more likely to ask God to bless our lives than to use us as blessings in the lives of others. We have all been guilty to some degree of being self-focused until the pastor preaches a sermon on selfishness, and then we willingly change our focus to others! "I sure wish so and so was here to hear this. She needs it!"

While it might be natural for us to look out for number one, Christians have a different call. When we choose to be followers of Jesus Christ, He calls us to dispel the notion that it's all about us. Yet the temptation to put ourselves first will always remain. The desires of the flesh and the desires of the Holy Spirit wage war against each other from the moment we pray to receive Christ. My way. His way. His way. My way. It is a constant battle. The goal is to come to a point where an attitude of "my way or the highway" becomes "His way is the high way."

The Greatest Love of All

Whitney Houston's song, "The Greatest Love of All," earned the number 2 spot on the Top 40 charts for 1986. She became a superstar almost overnight. Unfortunately, Whitney's fame, fortune, and pledge to love herself did little to help her overcome a drug problem that haunted her in the years that followed. How sad that she grew up singing in the church choir but failed to discover the greatest Love of all and to experience His love to the fullest.

The world may send a message to look out for number one, but God's Word sends a different message. Read Philippians 2:3-4 and fill in the blanks:

"Do nothing out of selfish ambition or vain conceit, but in

__________________ consider others __________________ than yourselves. Each of you should look not only to your own interests,

but also to the interests of __________________."

How does this passage differ from the world's message?

____

To act in selfish ambition is to seek to outdo others by elevating ourselves. Striving for personal excellence means being responsible stewards of the gifts we have been given. In both cases we seek to excel, but only in the latter is the motive of the heart pure.

Describe a time when you acted in selfish ambition.

____

In your opinion, is selfish ambition sometimes a problem in ministry?
❑ Yes ❑ No Explain your answer.

____

One Saturday afternoon I was watching my sons play football on the front lawn. They gathered boys from the neighborhood and split into teams. On one particular play, the ball was thrown to my eight-year-old son, Hayden, who dodged his opponents and charged into the end zone to score. Upon scoring, he proceeded to emulate the behavior of many of the professional football players on TV. He danced. He jaunted. He moon-walked. He jeered his opponents. It wasn't pretty. I feared for his life, given the fact he was the youngest one out there. What he did next topped it all. He ended his show by kneeling on one knee, bowing as if in prayer, and pointing up to God as if to say, "This is for You!" It was a perfect picture of vain conceit. Do our actions seek to bring glory to ourselves or to God?

Can you think of a time when you acted in vain conceit and sought glory for yourself rather than for God? Describe the situation.

____

____

According to Philippians 2:4, what virtue will enable us to consider others

as better than ourselves? ________________________________

The best model for humility is Christ. Read Philippians 2:5-8. What evidence can you cite to show that Christ thought more highly of others?

____

I am amazed that Christ, in His divinity and perfection, would treat sinners as better than Himself. Humility is only possible when we focus on our own faults and deficiencies rather than the faults and weaknesses of others.

In 1 Timothy 1:15, how did Paul refer to himself? ________________

In the *King James Version,* Paul refers to himself as "chief" of all sinners. Even some 2000 years later Paul is considered perhaps the greatest Christian, yet he referred to himself as "chief" of all sinners. The closer he grew to Christ, the more aware he became of his own deficiencies.

This is a faithful saying, and worthy of all acceptation, that Christ Jesus came into the world to save sinners; of whom I am chief.
–1 Timothy 1:15, KJV

Read the verse in the margin out loud, claiming it for yourself.

If you compared yourself to other sinners, and thought, "I know I'm a sinner, but there are other people who better qualify for 'chief' of all sinners," you missed the point. Only when you focus on the condition of your own heart is it possible to treat others as better than yourself.

If we are called to consider others as better than ourselves, what is the balance when it comes to love of self? We are created in His image. It is an insult to our Creator not to love His creation. However, He never intended for our love of self to supercede our love for Him or others.

What is the greatest commandment mentioned in Mark 12:28-31?

____

What is the second most important commandment?

____

What is one truth you would draw from the Scripture you've studied today?

____

____

____

____

Notice the logical order of progression. If we love God first and foremost, we will love ourselves as His unique creations. In turn, if we love ourselves as His unique creations, we will love and treat others as unique creations of God.

Write 1 John 4:19 in the margin.

For years, when I prayed for my children I prayed for their future spouses. I had a whole wish list of qualities that I prayed for regarding these spouses. I have since done away with my wish list and resorted to one thing: "Lord Jesus, if my child is called to marry, let his or her spouse love You more than they could ever love my child."

In closing, thank God for the ability to love others because He first loved you. Ask Him to help you consider others as better than yourself.

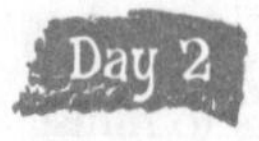

Outta This World

Several years ago my daughter Paige (eight years old at the time) had an opportunity to audition for a part in a movie. The movie had a cast of well-known actors and actresses, and Paige was asked to audition for the daughter of one of the lead actresses. The casting director had already seen her head shot and indicated that she had a strong chance of getting the part due to her small size and previous acting experience. This was her first opportunity to audition for a feature-length movie with a well-known celebrity cast.

As a responsible parent, I requested to review the content before the audition. Unfortunately, I did not receive the script until the night before the audition. As I read it, my heart grieved over blasphemous scenes, and my husband and I knew we could not allow our daughter to be in such a movie.

I shared with Paige that we would honor our commitment to attend the audition and then politely tell the casting director our decision not to audition for the part and the reasons for our decision. As you would imagine, our decision was met with modern-day persecution and shock that we would give up an opportunity for such a prominent part.

As Paige and I walked out after the appointment, we were practically skipping with joy. I explained to my young daughter that as Christians, we are called to march to the beat of a different drummer. I told her that throughout her life she would face many situations where she would be required to choose Jesus or the world. "Today," I told her, "we chose Jesus." As she gets older, I hope she will come to the conclusion that nothing is worth compromising her faith. I want my daughter to know that money and fame don't bring happiness. True happiness comes when we choose Jesus over the world.

Can you think of a time when you chose Jesus over the world?
❑ Yes ❑ No If yes, how did you feel?

____

Can you recall a time when you failed to choose Jesus over the world?
❑ Yes ❑ No If yes, how did that feel?

____

From the time we are young, we are expected to fit in and find our place. We want people to like us. We want to belong. The world is our home. Yet when we become Christians the world ceases to be our home. God give us a new home, a new mission, and a new identity. Because we have all conformed to the world to some degree, we find the process of transformation difficult. Some Christians will make the transition; unfortunately, most will not. Becoming a Christian is easy; living the Christian life is the most challenging thing you will ever do.

Romans 12:2 presents one of the biggest challenges to Christians. The verse is life-changing. Memorize it. Chant it like a mantra. Teach it to your children. Live it in your home.

Do not conform any longer to the pattern of this world, but be transformed by the renewing of your mind. Then you will be able to test and approve what God's will is–his good, pleasing and perfect will.
–Romans 12:2

God didn't expect us to "be transformed" just on Sundays. The secret to transformation? Renewing our minds. The Greek word for *renew* is *anakainosis* (an-ak-ah'-ee-no-sis) which means *renovation.* To renovate something is to replace the old with the new. The finished product should look newer and better. Part of replacing the old mindset with the new mindset is acknowledging that we are no longer in charge of our lives.

Read the following verses and write down what each says about your relationship with the world.

Scripture	My Relationship to the World
John 17:14-16	______________________________
Hebrews 13:14	______________________________
James 4:4	______________________________
1 Peter 2:11-12	______________________________
1 John 2:15-17	______________________________

For Christians, the Holy Spirit is the gauge that allows us to distinguish the world's ways from God's ways. He will convict our hearts when we are marching to the world's rat-a-tat-tat, and lovingly prompt us to march to His drumbeat. Unfortunately, many of us are not in the habit of listening for the Spirit's prompting.

List three times when the Holy Spirit has convicted you that He wants to change something in your life.

1. ______________________________________

2. ______________________________________

3. ______________________________________

How did you respond to the Holy Spirit's promptings in those instances?

1. ______________________________

2. ______________________________

3. ______________________________

How do you recognize the Holy Spirit's direction? (Check all that apply.)

❑ A feeling of conviction ❑ A Scripture speaks to me
❑ Something another believer says ❑ Pressure from a circumstance
❑ Other ____________________

We are called to seek out the good, pleasing, and perfect will of God. No more marching to the world's drumbeat. Close in prayer and ask God to help you choose Jesus over the world.

What is one truth you would draw from the Scripture you've studied today?

____

____

____

____

The Big Makeover: Before and After

Transformation is a life-long makeover. Mine began in 1985 and I still have a long way to go. If you don't believe me, just show up at one of my boys' football or basketball games. If the official makes an unfair call, I am pacing on the sidelines and blurting out comments. God called me on the carpet last year at a basketball game. The official made one horrible call after another. I was pacing. I was ranting. A mother from the other team came up to me and asked, "Are you Vicki Courtney?" After a long, pregnant pause, I stuttered, "Yes." She then shared, "We are doing your *Virtuous Woman* Bible study at my church and I'm really enjoying it." I was speechless. I was embarrassed. That day I vowed to change, and I can honestly say I'm getting better. Now, if the officials make unfair calls, you will find me in my car breathing heavily into a paper sack. It's a start.

Many people think being a Christian is easy. You acknowledge that Jesus died for your sins, say a prayer, and, poof, you're in the club. Not hardly. Becoming a Christian is more like signing up for major surgery.

List the characteristics of the old self and the new self from Ephesians 4:21-32.

Old Self	New Self

Read Colossians 3:5-10. Add these characteristics of the old self and new self in the columns above. Circle any characteristic of the old self you currently struggle with.

We are no longer slaves

to ________________.

We have been freed

from ________________.

Look up Romans 6:6-7 and fill in the blanks in the margin.

God has equipped us with power to say no to sin. Will we utilize the power He offers us? Will we agree to let Him perform surgery on our old nature? Becoming a Christian removes the penalty for our sin but does not remove the consequences that stem from them.

What are some consequences you have experienced from past sin?

____

Give a specific example of a recent occurrence when you struggled with one of the old self characteristics you circled. If God lays something else on your heart that was not mentioned, note that as well.

____

____

What can you do to stop the struggle in this area? (Check all that apply.)

- ❑ Give up
- ❑ Surrender to Christ
- ❑ Get an accountability partner
- ❑ Daily feed on God's Word
- ❑ Eat more liver
- ❑ Draw strength from other believers
- ❑ Request prayer support
- ❑ Vitamins, vitamins, vitamins

Read Romans 8:5-8 and fill in the blanks below.

"Those who live according to the sinful nature have their minds set on what that __________________ desires; but those who live in accordance with the Spirit have their minds set on what the __________________ desires. The mind of sinful man is __________________ but the mind controlled by the Spirit is __________________ and __________________."

The abundant life is a mind controlled by the Spirit, not by fleshly desires. Would you say you strive for a life controlled by the Holy Spirit? Do you have your mind set on what the Spirit desires?

The first verse I memorized as a Christian was 2 Corinthians 5:17. I am a new creation. Out with the old, in with the new. Does this mean I stopped sinning? Not exactly. But, I have the Spirit of Christ who gives me the power to say no to sin and convicts me when I do sin.

If anyone is in Christ, he is a new creation; the old has gone, the new has come!
–2 Corinthians 5:17

What must we do to be cleansed of all unrighteousness (1 John 1:9, KJV)?

____

One of the reasons I believe Alcoholics Anonymous is such a success is because they encourage members to acknowledge their problem by admitting, "I am an alcoholic." Many Christians struggle with their old self because they refuse to acknowledge we have an ongoing sin problem. We need to develop the ability to talk openly with God–and sometimes each other–about our specific areas of weakness.

He who conceals his sins
does not prosper,
but whoever confesses
and renounces them
finds mercy.
–Proverbs 28:13

Read the following verses and note the benefits to confessing your sins.

Scripture	Benefits
Proverbs 28:13	______________________________
James 5:16	______________________________

Confess your sins to each other and pray for each other so that you may be healed. The prayer of a righteous man is powerful and effective.
–James 5:16

What does Proverbs 28:13 say will happen if we conceal our sins?

____

Is there sin in your life that you are concealing? If so, stop and acknowledge it to God. Be specific! Ask God to send you a godly individual to whom you can confess your sin.

Why do you think it could be healing to confess your sins to another person (Jas. 5:16)?

____

The original Greek word for *confess* is *exomologeo* (ex-om-ol-og-eh'-o) and it means *to acknowledge or agree fully.* The original Greek word for *heal* is *iaomai* (ee-ah'-om-ahee) and it means *to cure (literally or figuratively).* Oh, the sins that could be cured if we would own them and confess them! When we acknowledge our sin, we admit we have a problem. When we acknowledge our sin to another, it strengthens our understanding of God's grace, and drains the power from the sinful behavior.

Can you think of a time when you acknowledged a particular sin struggle to another person and it produced healing? Share your story below.

____

____

What is one truth you would draw from the Scripture you've studied today?

____

____

____

____

Note that God allowed the apostle Paul to continue to struggle with a "thorn in the flesh" (see 2 Cor. 12:7). Confession will generally produce healing, but sometimes God desires greater glory by allowing struggle in our lives. Don't let apparent failure discourage you. Remember Galatians 6:9: "Let us not become weary in doing good, for at the proper time we will reap a harvest if we do not give up."

Close in prayer, asking God to help you improve in the areas where you still struggle with the old self. Claim Philippians 1:6: "Being confident of this, that he who began a good work in you will carry it on to completion until the day of Christ Jesus." The Great Physician will not complete the surgery until we breathe our last breath.

Day 4

The Happiness Myth: God Wants Me to be Happy!

Several years ago I was talking with a friend who had left her husband and was filing for divorce. She was active in church and Bible studies. Her husband was an agnostic for years, and it caused a strain on their marriage. My friend had prayed for her husband's salvation over the years and had asked my husband and me to pray, as well. Finally, her prayers were answered. Her husband had recently become a Christian and was growing rapidly in his newfound faith. However, it was too little, too late for my friend. The conversation was strained as I asked her why she was leaving her husband. She said, "I'm glad he's found Christ, but it doesn't erase the unhappy years in our marriage. I feel confident that my decision to divorce is in God's will. The Jesus I believe in would not want me to remain in an unhappy marriage. He would want me to be happy."

The last I checked, the Jesus I believe in traded His own personal happiness for death on a cross. Christians often mistakenly assume their life mission is the pursuit of happiness. Many Christians pursue earthly pleasures strictly forbidden by God in an effort to achieve perceived happiness. We are fortunate that Jesus was not concerned with happiness when He prayed in Gethsemane and said, " 'My Father, if it is possible, may this cup be taken from me. Yet not as I will, but as you will' " (Matt. 26:39). Just prior to His plea to God, He said to His disciples, " 'My soul is overwhelmed with sorrow to the point of death' " (Matt. 26:38). Hardly a picture of euphoria or happiness. We forget that Jesus was fully human and had every opportunity to trade doing good for feeling good. How dare we minimize our Savior's death by falsely assuming that He died for our happiness. He died for our forgiveness.

Contrary to the view of many Christians, God has never condoned feeling good over doing good. God is much more concerned with our obedience than our personal happiness.

Look up the following verses and note what obedience implies.

John 14:15 ____

John 14:23-24 ____

Romans 2:13-14 ____

1 John 5:1-5____

There are times when we knowingly choose feeling good over doing good. Does that mean we don't love God?

When I knowingly disobey God's Word, I still love God. The conviction of the Holy Spirit causes misery in my heart over my wrongdoing. This conviction eventually leads me to agree with God that what I did was wrong and I repent. Repentance should always be followed by changed behavior. The danger is failing to respond to the conviction that God places on our hearts. We send a message that says, "I love myself more than I love God."

What area(s) do you struggle with most in regard to obedience?

____

How have you responded to conviction over these area(s) of sin?

____

Rather than happiness, what does obedience lead to (John 15:10-11)?

____

The Greek word for *joy* is *chara* (khar-ah') which means *cheerfulness or calm delight.* Joy is a fruit of the Holy Spirit. Joy lasts while happiness is usually a temporary and fleeting state. Joy does not depend on happiness, while happiness does depend on joy. Joy can be felt in the most dismal of times and can bring a calm delight to the soul. The abundant life is a life full of joy, not happiness.

In days 2 and 3 we established that God expects us to be set apart from the world and be different. Yet we can all think of Christians who, in spite of these truths, are still holding hands with the world. Why is it so hard for some to break away from the ways of the world and be different? Are they mainly interested in the long-term benefits of heaven without having to take up the cross of Christ and follow Him?

Perhaps you don't have a desire to give it all up to follow Christ. Maybe you didn't realize that there was more to it than saying a prayer of salvation or being confirmed in your church. Perhaps you don't desire to be different. You like this world. You like the way you are. That line of thinking is really saying, "It's all about me." Christianity was never intended to be all about us, but rather, all about Him. When God allowed His only Son to die on a cross for our sins, in a sense

He said, "This is all about you." However, His intention was to provoke a response from us that says, "Wow. What a gift! In gratitude of this tremendous gift, I am willing to serve my God rather than myself."

Have you moved past "It's all about me," to "It's all about Him"? In closing, read 1 John 2:3-6. Pray as God leads.

What is one truth you would draw from the Scripture you've studied today?

____

____

____

____

Dying to Live

On December 10, 1997, Julia Hill climbed 180 feet into the upper boughs of an ancient redwood tree and refused to come down. Her tree-sit was in defiance of plans to cut the tree down. During her tree-sit, she endured the stormiest, coldest winter in Northern California's recorded history. It was 2 years and 8 days before her feet touched the ground again. When she finally came down she collapsed in a ball, weeping. After a long moment, she rose to her knees, lifted her arms up toward the tree, and cried out, "We did it!"

Too bad Julia Hill has mistakenly chosen to worship the creation rather than the Creator. We could use someone with that kind of passion standing firm for the cause of Christ. While Julia Hill gave up two years of her life to save a tree, many Christians can't seem to give up two hours a week to attend church and worship the Creator of the tree. How sad! While Julia Hill passionately shares her earth-friendly message, many of us are trying to work up the nerve to share Christ with our hairdresser.

Today we will look at what it means to surrender our lives to Christ. Don't worry, it doesn't require sitting in a tree. It's much worse. It requires dying.

Read the following verses. List that to which we are dead and alive.

Scripture	Dead	Alive
Romans 6:11	_______________	_______________
Romans 8:10	_______________	_______________
Ephesians 2:1-6	_______________	_______________

Do the verses call us to die a physical death? ❑ Yes ❑ No

"As long as you did what you felt like doing, ignoring God, you didn't have to bother with right thinking or right living, or right anything for that matter. But do you call that a free life? What did you get out of it? Nothing you're proud of now. Where did it get you? A dead end. But now that you've found you don't have to listen to sin tell you what to do, and have discovered the delight of listening to God telling you, what a surprise! A whole, healed, put-together life right now, with more and more of life on the way! Work hard for sin your whole life and your pension is death. But God's gift is real life, eternal life, delivered by Jesus, our Master."
–Romans 6:16-23, *The Message*

If we are dead to sin, why do we continue to sin?

____

What does Romans 6:11-14 say we should offer to God?

____

Many Christians will miss out on the abundant life because they refuse to offer their entire being to God. Some reason, "Look God, I give You one day a week at church, I read my Bible occasionally, we talk from time to time. Isn't that enough? You can have all of me … well, except the part of me that ______ (is bitter, likes to gossip, lies, lusts for material things, commits adultery, refuses to forgive others, seeks worldly approval, overeats, drinks excessively, judges others, and so on).

A friend of mine recently shared a disturbing conversation she had with her hairdresser. The subject of church came up in their conversation and her hairdresser professed to be a Christian. He also professed to be gay. He spoke openly of his adoration for Jesus Christ and admitted that he knew the Bible was clear regarding homosexuality. He claimed that it would be as unnatural for him to be heterosexual as it would be for a heterosexual to be homosexual. He shared with my friend that he attended church, prayed, and read his Bible often. He believed that a loving God would not expect him to spend his life without the companionship of another human being. He concluded that in spite of his sin, Jesus had forgiven him. Talk about taking grace for granted!

Let's take his brand of cheap grace a step further. To the Christian woman in an unhappy marriage who meets a man who makes her heart beat faster, go for it! To the Christian couple who desire to live together outside of marriage, shack up! To the Christian who wants to move to a bigger home but can't afford it if he or she tithes, pack up and move! To the Christian who dulls inner pain with food, eat up! To the Christian who turns to alcohol in times of distress, drink up! To the Christian teenager who wishes to satisfy raging hormones, sleep around! Go for it, Christians! If it feels good, do it! You're forgiven!

Romans 6:14 explains that Christians are no longer under law, but under grace. This means that it doesn't matter what Christians do, right? Wrong! My friend's hairdresser has refused to die fully to sin. He may believe in Jesus, but he is not alive to Jesus. He elevated his need for human companionship above obedience to God. How sad that he could not imagine a full and abundant life apart from his fleshly desires. In answer to his statement that "God would not want him to spend his life without the companionship of another human being," guess what? If such companionship involves sin, He would. God never said it would be easy to be a Christ-follower. Many Christians have a hard time with that concept because we are not used to being told no by anyone, including God. Although God tells us no for our good, we would often rather believe the world's lies that answering yes will lead to happiness.

Read Romans 6:15 from your Bible. Now read it again in first person.

According to Romans 6:16, what happens to a person who answers yes to that question?

____

Our options are not between obedience to God and a life of fun. Our choices are submission to God or slavery to sin.

The abundant life is impossible unless we say no to sin and yes to God. We can only do so when we offer every ounce of our being to God as a living sacrifice. I wonder if we hesitate to offer ourselves as living sacrifices to God because we are afraid He might take us up on it. What if I am called to a third world country to proclaim the gospel? What if I turn into a Jesus freak and my friends think I've gone nuts? What if I have to lead a Bible study? So what?

Close today in prayer, asking God to help you come to the end of yourself and live for the real number one, Jesus Christ.

What is one truth you would draw from the Scripture you've studied today?

____

____

____

____

Truth to Go

It may be human nature to look out for number one, but Christians have a higher call. We are called to dispel the notion that it's all about us. When we become Christians, Jesus assumes the number one spot. The temptation to put ourselves first will always remain. The desires of the flesh and the desires of the Holy Spirit will wage war constantly.

The abundant life becomes ours only when we come to the end of ourselves and live for Christ. The abundant life involves scrapping the attitude of "my way or the highway" and believing "His way is the high way"!

Week 6

I'll Have the All-You-Can-Eat Buffet

Myth #6: I can have it all.

I collect old magazines. When I flip through the pages of magazines 50 or more years old, I am amazed at the many references to the Christian faith. For example, in the February, 1900 edition of *Ladies' Home Journal,* an article addresses modern women concerned with money and success. The article refers to modern women belonging to "a generation of busy Marthas," and asks the question, "Has she time to rock her baby to sleep with Bible stories?"[1] The writer of the article clearly assumed that women reading the *Journal* would know the Martha of Luke 10:38-42.

Today any mention of Martha in a women's magazine would most likely be in reference to Martha Stewart. Rather than extol the virtues of rocking your baby to sleep, the article would likely cover how to make the rocker from scratch by carving an oak tree you planted and grew in your well-groomed front lawn.

My, how times have changed! References to Christianity in magazine articles today are most often negative portrayals of our faith. Flipping through the pages of magazines from times long past often leaves me with conflicting emotions. On one hand, I am nostalgic and envious of a time when most parents raised their children to believe in God, church, and country. On the other hand, I am relieved to live in the era of microwaves, dishwashers, and Lunchables.

Today our country is feasting on a giant buffet of different religions and belief systems. Christianity, once the main entrée, is now one of many entrées offered in the buffet line. Only one faith can completely satisfy the hunger pangs of a culture craving meaning in life. Only one faith will lead to a relationship with God. Only one faith will result in the abundant life. That faith is Christianity.

Christians must know their roots. They must know what they signed up for when they became Christians. Further, they must live with direction and purpose. Christians who are experiencing the abundant life should refuse to experience it alone. It fact, it ceases to be abundant if it is not shared. Are you doing your part to ensure that the flickering flame of Christianity is not extinguished for future generations?

Who Do You Say He Is?

He was not born into royalty or power, yet He was the most powerful man to ever live. He never wrote a book, but His words are recorded in the best-selling book of all time. During His life, He never raised up an army, but an estimated 330,000 people are martyred for His cause each year. Even our current calendar system stems from His birth, recognizing two time periods, B.C. (before Christ) and A.D. (Anno Domini, "the year of our Lord").

Hundreds of years before He was born, His appearance was spoken of in over 300 prophecies recorded in the Old Testament. Even His death did not quench the curiosity surrounding His life. Some 2000 years later, He continues to impact the world more than anyone else who ever lived. Who is He? Jesus Christ, of course.

Today those who claim to be His followers number approximately 1.9 billion throughout the world. One-third of the world's population professes to be Christian. Without Jesus Christ, Christianity would cease to exist. Other world religions were established on the philosophical propositions of a founding prophet. Take the prophet away from such religions and they would remain intact. Christianity, on the other hand, rests entirely on the person of Jesus Christ and who He claimed to be. Take Jesus away, and Christianity falls.

In this last week of our study we'll face the prevailing attitude of our day–that Jesus is one offering of many on the religious buffet line. How do we deal with the exclusivism of Christianity? Is Jesus the only way to God or do all roads lead to heaven?

When Jesus asked His disciples, " 'Who do people say the Son of Man is?' " how did they answer (Matt. 16:13-20)?

❑ John the Baptist ❑ Elijah
❑ Jeremiah ❑ One of the prophets
❑ All of these

What question did Jesus then pose to the disciples? ____________________

____

Who answered and what was his answer?______________________________

____

Do you agree with Peter? ❑ Yes ❑ No

In John 4:25-26, Jesus converses with a Samaritan woman who originally speculated that He was a prophet. When she referred to the coming Messiah, Jesus responded with, " 'I who speak to you am he.' " The Samaritan woman had heard of the rumored Messiah to come. Now, she stood before Him.

There is no doubt that Jesus is the Son of God, but is Jesus God? Read the following verses and write down the relationship of Jesus to God.

Scripture	Relationship
John 1:1	________________________
John 1:14	________________________
John 1:18	________________________
John 10:30	________________________
John 14:9	________________________
1 John 2:23	________________________

The Bible clearly shows that to know God, the Father, one must know Jesus, the Son of God. Jesus is not merely a prophet or a teacher. Jesus is God in the form of a man. He was God made flesh. He was fully God and fully man.

No man hath seen God at any time; the only begotten Son, which is in the bosom of the Father, he hath declared him.
–John 1:18, KJV

Was Jesus present with God from the beginning of time? ❑ Yes ❑ No

John 1:18 (in the margin) dispels any speculation that Jesus was a mere prophet, teacher, or man. Jesus was with God the Father from the beginning of time. He rested in the bosom of the Father. He knew God fully. Prophets were given the task of delivering messages from God to the people. When on earth, Jesus declared to mankind what He knew of God, firsthand.

According to Matthew 26:63-64, what was the charge the Pharisees brought against Jesus?

____

Did Jesus admit to being the Christ, the Son of God? ❑ Yes ❑ No

C. S. Lewis, the famous writer who converted from atheism to Christianity, said:

> I'm trying here to prevent anyone from saying the really silly thing that people often say about Him: "I'm ready to accept Jesus as a great moral teacher, but I don't accept His claim to be God." That's the one thing we mustn't say. A man who was merely man and said the sort of things Jesus said wouldn't be a great moral teacher. He'd either be a lunatic–on a level with the man who says he is a poached egg–or else he'd be the Devil of Hell. You must make your choice. Either this man was, and is, the Son of God: or else a madman or something worse. You can shut Him up for a fool, you can spit at Him and kill Him as a demon; or you can fall at His feet and call Him Lord and God. But don't let us come with any patronising {sic} nonsense about His being a great human teacher. He hasn't left that open to us. He didn't intend to.[2]

What is one truth you would draw from the Scripture you've studied today?

____

____

____

____

You may wonder why I am covering the basics of Christianity. You might be surprised how few professing Christians know the basics. Tomorrow I will share some supporting statistics that will knock your socks off. Without a basic understanding of who Jesus is, it is impossible to tell others who He is. Every Christian should be able to articulate to others who Jesus claims to be.

Gone are the days when most everyone we meet is a Bible-knowing and Bible-believing Christian. As a result, people are confused about who Jesus Christ is and the basic tenets of Christianity. Unfortunately, the confusion is not exclusive to non-Christians, but is prevalent among Christians as well.

In the end, each of us will have to answer the question Jesus posed to His disciples, "Who do you say I am?" There will only be one right answer. Our eternal destiny will depend on the answer we give. Close today by answering Jesus' question, "Who do you say I am?"

Is Christianity Politically Correct?

"Christians are so narrow-minded!" I'm sure you've heard that before. The truth that Jesus is the only way to God is usually what brands Christianity as narrow-minded, intolerant, and politically incorrect.

I recently had a conversation with a man who professed to be a Christian, yet had reservations about Jesus Christ being the only way to heaven. He said something to the effect of, "I can't imagine that a loving God would purposely exclude others who seek to know Him but choose a different means than Christ. You don't really believe that Jesus is the only way to heaven, do you?"

I shared with him that when I professed a belief in Jesus Christ, I signed up to be a follower of Jesus Christ. As a follower, I committed to live by the standards set forth in God's Word. The Bible became my guidebook for living and my compass for discerning truth. I shared that the Bible is clear that there is only one way to reach God and it is through His Son, Jesus Christ. I reminded him that I didn't make up the rules, God did. Then I asked him, "Why would someone who claims to be a follower of Christ not believe Christ's claim that He is the way, the truth, and the life and that no man can come to the Father, but through Him?" (see John 14:6) He didn't have an answer. And this man regularly attends church!

How would you have responded to his statement?

- ❑ Nice weather we're having. I hear a cold front is blowing in this weekend.
- ❑ Are you nuts? I thought you said you were a Christian!
- ❑ What kind of wacky church do you attend? You just made my prayer list!
- ❑ A response similar to mine.

Based on an article by the Barna Research Group entitled, "Americans' Bible Knowledge Is In the Ballpark, But Often Off Base," the response of this man is not all that shocking. A nationwide survey done in 2000 produced some disturbing results. Many born-again Christians hold beliefs that are contrary to the Bible. For example, 68 percent of born-again Christians believe the Bible teaches that God helps those who help themselves; 53 percent believe the Holy Spirit does not exist; 47 percent believe Satan does not exist; 31 percent believe a person can earn his or her way to heaven by being good; 30 percent believe that Jesus died but was not physically resurrected, 26 percent believe it doesn't matter what faith you follow because they all teach the same lessons. Perhaps the most disturbing result was that a whopping 24 percent of born-again Christians believe that Jesus committed sins![3] Clearly, many Christians do not know the basics of Christianity.

On the other hand, those who know the basics of Christianity are often hesitant to defend their faith for fear they will appear intolerant of beliefs held by others. God never called Christians to be tolerant of other faiths. Luke 12:49-53 tells what Jesus would say to those concerned with tolerance.

Did Jesus come to bring peace on earth? ❑ Yes ❑ No

If not peace, then what?______________________________

Division! He sounds anything but tolerant. Should you encounter someone who believes that many paths lead to heaven or one of the 26 percent of born-again Christians who say it doesn't matter what faith you follow, take note of the verses in the margin.

Jesus answered, "I am the way and the truth and the life. No one comes to the Father except through me."
–John 14:6

Salvation is found in no one else, for there is no other name under heaven given to men by which we must be saved.
–Acts 4:12

Jesus had no concern for being politically correct. I can't imagine the number of opportunities to share the gospel that Christians have missed for fear of being labeled intolerant. I am not encouraging Christians to get in fights concerning the faith. We will discuss proper presentation of the gospel on day 4, but first it is necessary to dispel the world's mindset regarding tolerance. Tolerate can be defined as: "to neither forbid or prevent: permit." If someone states a belief that is contrary to a truth in the Bible, to nod our heads in agreement or say nothing at all is to tolerate or permit someone to believe a falsehood.

While we need to respect other's beliefs when discussing spiritual truths and treat people with kindness, we are remiss if we say nothing when a falsehood is spoken. If someone believed he or she could jump out of an airplane without a parachute and land safely on the ground, would we remain silent? Of course not! Why, then, would we hesitate to speak up when someone claims that many paths lead to heaven? If we respond with silence (or worse, nod in agreement), one could easily come to the conclusion that his or her belief is valid and acceptable.

What two things does it take for someone to be saved (Rom. 10:9)?

1. ______________________ 2. ______________________

It is not acceptable to believe in Jesus yet deny that God raised Him from the dead. When someone challenges a Christian on the validity of the resurrection of Jesus Christ, it is a simple argument. First of all, Jesus foretold His death and resurrection in Luke 18:31-33. Secondly, if Jesus never resurrected from the dead, why did the remaining 11 disciples go on to risk their lives to preach the gospel? Many went on to die for their faith and all were severely persecuted. Not one, when standing in the face of persecution or death, would retract his testimony concerning Christ. These are the same fellows who deserted Christ before His resurrection and were fearful after His death. What transformed the disciples into zealous preachers of the gospel? The resurrection! After the resurrection, Christ appeared at least 10 times to those who had known Him.

Do you believe that Christ resurrected from the dead? ❑ Yes ❑ No
How would you respond to someone who questions the resurrection?

____

____

After an exhaustive examination of the evidence given for the resurrection of Christ, Simon Greenleaf, cofounder of the Harvard Graduate School of Law, said: "It was therefore impossible that they could have persisted in affirming the truths they have narrated, had not Jesus actually risen from the dead, and had they not known this fact as certainly as they knew any other fact."[4] His conclusion led him to accept Christ as His Savior. He went on to write *Testimony of the Evangelists,* in which he stated that the Bible stood every test of evidence a court of law could impose. He even encouraged members of the legal profession to examine the legitimacy of the resurrection. And to think that approximately 30 percent of born-again Christians claim not to believe in the physical resurrection of Christ! The resurrection sets Christ apart from all other prophets. The other prophets can be found in their graves. Christianity rests on the resurrection of Jesus Christ. He was able to overcome death because He was divine.

Entire books on the validity of Christianity support the life, death, and resurrection of Jesus Christ. It would be impossible for me to do the topic justice in a few short pages. However, my goal is to whet your appetite to follow up with more study. If we truly desire to pass on the abundant life to others, we must first be able to share the source of the abundant life.

Close today and ask God to equip you to stand for Christ in the days to come. Share with Him any hesitation or insecurities you are feeling. Ask Him to provide you with boldness to proclaim His truths.

What is one truth you would draw from the Scripture you've studied today?

____

____

____

____

Day 3

Are You a Good Soldier?

In the presence of God and of Christ Jesus, who will judge the living and the dead, and in view of his appearing and his kingdom, I give you this charge: Preach the Word; be prepared in season and out of season; correct, rebuke and encourage–with great patience and careful instruction. For the time will come when men will not put up with sound doctrine. Instead, to suit their own desires, they will gather around them a great number of teachers to say what their itching ears want to hear. They will turn their ears away from the truth and turn aside to myths. But you, keep your head in all situations, endure hardship, do the work of an evangelist, discharge all the duties of your ministry.
–2 Timothy 4:1-5

Today we will talk about our duty as Christians to share Christ (the Author of the abundant life) with others. It is not an option but a charge.

In 2 Timothy 2:3-4, Paul cautions Timothy to be a "good soldier of Christ." A soldier is set apart for a specific mission and has a duty to report to a commanding officer. On the other hand, a civilian is a member of the general population and not required to report for duty. As I write this, our President has deployed soldiers to Afghanistan and throughout the world to fight the war on terrorism. We'd be in a heap of trouble if our soldiers refused to follow orders and took up civilian activities by doing their own will their own way.

List 2-3 civilian activities Christians commonly practice. Stick with offenses that deviate from standards of conduct set forth in God's Word.

____

____

Stop for a moment and pray. Ask God to reveal to you anything in your own life that might constitute a civilian activity and list it below.

____

____

In 2 Timothy 4:1-5 in the margin, underline any active charge Paul gives to Timothy in his call to be a good soldier.

The first charge Paul gave was to preach the Word. The original Greek word for *preach* is *kerusso* (kay-roos'-so), which means *to herald as a public crier.* It is the duty of every good soldier to herald the Word of God. It would make sense that to preach the Word, we must first know the Word. Unfortunately, as we discovered in yesterday's lesson, many Christians are desperately lacking knowledge of God's Word. For Christians to be good soldiers, we must first recognize we need to get into God's Word as basic training for the battles that lie ahead.

Where would you rank yourself on your knowledge of the Word?

1	5	10
How do you find Genesis?		I've memorized Habakkuk.

Where would you rank yourself on relaying the truths of the Bible to others?

1	5	10
Mums the word		Share regularly

After Paul exhorts Timothy to preach the Word, he warns him to "be prepared in season and out of season; correct, rebuke and encourage–with great patience and careful instruction" (2 Tim. 4:2). A good soldier is never off duty. The true test will come when we face unexpected opportunities to tell others about God's truth. A good soldier is equipped and prepared for out-of-season occurrences.

In 2 Timothy 4:3-4, what warning does Paul give Timothy?

____

In your opinion, has this time come? ❑ Yes ❑ No If yes, give an example.

____

In the next verse, Paul charges Timothy as a good soldier to keep his head in all situations and endure hardship. A good soldier expects to encounter hardships from time to time while serving out his or her call. The enemy will do much to thwart a soldier's intended mission.

What hardships have you experienced while serving as a good soldier for Christ? List them in the margin.

Read 2 Timothy 3:12. What does it say regarding persecution?

____

If you could not list any occurrences where you have experienced persecution, you may have need for concern.

[18]All this is from God, who reconciled us to himself through Christ and gave us the ministry of reconciliation: [19]that God was reconciling the world to himself in Christ, not counting men's sins against them. And he has committed to us the message of reconciliation. [20]We are therefore Christ's ambassadors, as though God were making his appeal through us. We implore you on Christ's behalf: Be reconciled to God.
–2 Corinthians 5:18-20

Review 2 Timothy 4:1-5. Can you honestly say you have reported for duty as a good soldier? ❑ Yes ❑ No If not, are you ready? ❑ Yes ❑ No

What does Jesus say in Matthew 5:11-12 regarding those who are persecuted

on His behalf? ____

What does Jesus say in John 17:14 about His prayer to the Father concerning persecution of His disciples?

____

The final charge Paul gives to Timothy appears at the end of 2 Timothy 4:5. Paul tells Timothy to "do the work of an evangelist, discharge all the duties of your ministry." Some Christians mistakenly believe that the call to evangelism is exclusively for paid ministers. All Christians are called to be evangelists. God entrusts each Christian with His gospel message. In addition, He has given each Christian a ministry. A good soldier's mission is to tell others the good news.

Answer the following questions based on 2 Corinthians 5:18-20.

What is our ministry (v. 18)? ______________________________

What do we tell others (v. 20)? ______________________________

What is our job title (v. 20)? ______________________________

What is one truth you would draw from the Scripture you've studied today?

____

____

____

____

We cannot fully experience the abundant life unless we tell others how they, too, can experience it. Only through Jesus Christ will one experience victory, so a Christian's mission is to show men and women the way of victory. In the end, I want to stand before my Commanding Officer wearing tattered and torn fatigues and my face covered with dirt and grime, fresh from the trenches of battle. On that day, I long to hear Him say, "Well done, soldier. You have fought the good fight." Victory, sweet victory.

Close today by asking God to help you fulfill the charge He has given you as a good soldier for Christ.

Day 4

Presentation Is Everything!

My grandmother survived bladder cancer and breast cancer before she received news that the cancer had spread to her brain. One month later, she was admitted to the hospital with complications. Tests revealed that the tumor had grown and multiplied, and she was given only days to live. As I sat by her bed in the days that followed, I watched her health deteriorate. Had there been a cure for this horrible disease, I would have done anything in my power to obtain it for her. I miss my grandmother terribly, but someday I will see her again in heaven.

In Mark 2, four men brought their paralyzed friend to Jesus in hopes that He would heal him. No doubt, they had heard rumors of His miraculous healing powers and felt it was the only hope for their friend.

In Mark 2:1-5, the men were determined to get their friend to Jesus. Can you imagine what the crowd thought with dirt sprinkling down on them as the men dug a hole in the earthen roof? And if that wasn't enough, what did the crowd think as the paralyzed man was lowered down on his mat? The men's persistence paid off because Jesus healed their friend.

What did Jesus say to the paralytic in Mark 2:5?

____

When Jesus saw their faith, he said to the paralytic, "Son, your sins are forgiven."
–Mark 2:5

How interesting that He chose the words "Your sins are forgiven" rather than "You have been healed."

What does Jesus say to the Pharisees in Mark 2:17?

____

"It is not the healthy who need a doctor, but the sick. I have not come to call the righteous, but sinners."
–Mark 2:17

Who represents the sick? ______________________________

Who represents the Doctor? ____________________________

Just as the four men faithfully took their friend to Jesus, we, too, are called to take our friends to the Great Physician. Sin is a fatal disease that will take every life eternally, but we know the Cure! A Christian's motivation for taking others to

Jesus is the knowledge that without the Cure, they will die in their sin. People are dying in their sin every day. A good soldier has a duty to introduce as many people as possible to the Great Physician.

1. ____________________

2. ____________________

3. ____________________

4. ____________________

5. ____________________

In the margin, list five people you know who need the Cure for their sins.

What word does Paul use to describe himself and Apollos in 1 Corinthians 3:5?

____

Fill in the blanks below.

"So neither he who ______________ nor he who ______________

is ______________, but only God, who makes things ______________.

The man who plants and the man who waters have one ______________, and each will be rewarded according to his own labor" (1 Cor 3:7-8).

When we tell others about Jesus, we plant seeds. Other times, we may be given the privilege of watering seeds that were previously planted by someone else. However, only God can make the seed grow. We must be sensitive to the opportunities God gives us to plant and water, but not feel pressure to do it all. We are not responsible for the end result–God is.

As a new Christian, I misunderstood my duty to tell others about Christ. In all my enthusiasm, I blasted many people with the gospel. I pray that Christ brought good from my honest intentions, in spite of my presentation. I was preachy, pushy, and sometimes argumentative. However, my actions were rooted in a sincere desire that no one go to hell. As I have matured as a Christian, I realize that as much as I care about others becoming Christians, God cares more. God can speak to the hearts of unbelievers in a variety of ways. He can certainly manage without me forcing my beliefs on them!

Read 2 Timothy 2:23-25 and answer these questions.

How should we respond to "foolish and stupid arguments" (v. 23)?

____

How should we respond to those who oppose us (v. 25)?

___

What two responses are described in Jude 22-23? ___

___

If we ask Him, God will be faithful to give us discernment through His Holy Spirit on how to approach each person. It is critical that we rely on Him to give us the words to say in each situation. We need to treat some people with mercy and patience, and others we need to literally "snatch from the fire." We must pray for opportunities to share Christ with others and be ready to open our mouths and speak the words the Holy Spirit provides when the time comes.

Read 1 Corinthians 2:1-5. What words did Paul use to describe how he was feeling when he brought the good news to the people of Corinth (v. 3)?

___

On what did he rely (v. 4)? ___

In Matthew 10:19-20 Jesus tells the people not to worry about what they will say. Why?

___

Describe a situation when the Spirit clearly gave you the words to say.

___

There will be times when you feel you could have said more to a person, while other times you may feel you said too much. Don't beat yourself up. Ask God to bring good from the situation and move on. The most important thing is that you make yourself available to God as a willing vessel. Trust Him for the details.

Close today by praying for each of the people you listed earlier who are in need of the Cure for their sin. Ask God to give you the opportunity and the boldness to share Jesus with them.

What is one truth you would draw from the Scripture you've studied today?

___

___

___

___

The Bread of Life

I can't believe our journey to get a life is almost over. I want to spend our last day reviewing the basic hindrances to the abundant life and taking time to do self-assessments regarding each one.

When I face adversity I emerge:

Bitter — Better

Myth #1: If I follow Christ, my life will be trouble free. The Lord was with Joseph and he prospered. You will not encounter adversity alone, but you will encounter adversity. The Lord is with you and desires to prosper you in spite of your adversity.

I seek to be loved and completed by:

A man — Christ

Myth #2: A man will make me happy. Only Jesus Christ can provide unconditional, unfailing, eternal love. The story of redemption is the greatest love story ever told.

Overall, I run the race at:

The world's pace — God's pace

Myth #3: A busy life = An abundant life. Run the race to be a champion, rather than merely a contestant. Champions take time to refuel with the Word and prayer. Champions focus on the finish line (Jesus) and run for an eternal prize.

When it comes to an attitude of gratitude, I am more in the habit of:

Forgetting all He has done — Remembering all He has done

Myth #4: Material possessions will lead to peace and purpose. Be content with what you have rather than focus on what you don't have. When you pray, make sure your desires match God's desires.

I look out for number one. Therefore, I seek to serve:

Myself God

Myth #5: It's all about me. Christians must allow God the number one spot. This world is only a stopping place on the timeline of eternity. Christians show our love for God by obeying Him. We must daily die to self and live for Christ.

I share the Source (Christ) of the abundant life:

Never Often

Myth #6: I can have it all. Who do you say He is? Christians must develop the ability to effectively communicate their beliefs with others.

Overall, how are you feeling about what we have discussed during this study regarding the pursuit of the abundant life?
❑ Too much effort. I'm satisfied with just a life.
❑ I'm going for it. You only live once.
❑ This is too good not to share!

What are two areas from the self-analysis that need improvement in your life?

1. ______________________________

2. ______________________________

What are your areas of strength according to the self-analysis?

1. ______________________________

2. ______________________________

3______________________________

If you are feeling overwhelmed with the pursuit of the abundant life, let me encourage you to persevere. The only reason I feel qualified to write a study on the pursuit of the abundant life is because I have experienced first-hand every hindrance addressed in this study. We cannot order the abundant life from the world's menu. The world's menu may satisfy for a time, but it cannot satisfy consistently or completely. In John 6:35, Jesus declared, " 'I am the bread of life.

He who comes to me will never go hungry, and he who believes in me will never be thirsty.' " Only the Bread of life will satisfy the hunger pangs for an abundant life.

The abundant life does not discriminate. It is available to everyone, regardless of circumstances. It cannot be squelched by adversity, duplicated by man, provided by the world, or experienced alone. Yet, in spite of its ready availability, few pursue it.

I count myself among the blessed ones, who, content with life, will someday retire from this world a satisfied guest. My satisfaction is not rooted in prosperity, achievements, knowledge, success, or even family. My satisfaction comes from Jesus Christ and Him alone. I do not walk with Christ for the end goal of obtaining the abundant life. Rather, I walk with Him for the pleasure of His company. My pursuit is not for the abundant life, but rather to know Christ, the Author of the abundant life. The abundant life comes as a natural by-product of a life closely aligned with Christ. Regardless of circumstance, my life is abundant, for no one can rob me of my Savior. He alone satisfies.

Truth to Go

What is one truth you would draw from the Scripture you've studied today?

____

____

____

____

Is Jesus just one offering of many on the religious buffet line? Is Jesus the only way to God or do all roads lead to heaven? I hope by now you realized that it is only through Jesus Christ one can experience victory.

If you set out to pursue the abundant life as your end goal, you will fail. If you set out to pursue Jesus, you will quickly realize that you have everything you need to experience a life exceedingly abundantly above what you ever hoped or imagined. No Jesus, no life. Know Jesus, know life. It's that simple. Now, go and … get a life!

---

[1]"Fifty Years Ago in the Journal," *Ladies Home Journal,* February 1950, 33.

[2]C.S. Lewis, *The Case for Christianity* (New York: Touchstone, 1996), 45.

[3]Americans' Bible Knowledge Is In the Ballpark, But Often Off Base," 12 July 2000, Barna Research Group, <*http://www.barna.org*>. Used by permission.

[4]Simon Greenleaf, *The Testimony of the Evangelists,* as found in John Warwick Montgomery, *Law About the Law* (Minneapolis, MN: Bethany Fellowship, 1975), 119.

Leader Guide

A small-group study of *Get a Life!* is appropriate for home groups, Bible-study groups, accountability groups, and discipleship groups. Get together at a time that works for your group. Sessions are planned to be one to one and one-half hours in length. However, allow the Holy Spirit to determine your schedule. I have supplied far more suggested questions than your group will have time to cover. Don't feel you have to cover them all. The plans in this leader guide serve as a framework; your goal should be to meet the needs of your group.

I recommend an introductory session to start the study, but if you do not have time for one, distribute the books at least one week in advance and start with session 1.

Before each group session, as group leader you should pray for each group member, study the material for the week, encourage those in the group, and get in touch quickly anytime someone misses a session.

God bless you as you facilitate your small group.

Introductory Session (optional)

Before the Session

- Gather markers and materials for making nametags for all persons attending.
- Obtain *Get a Life!* workbooks and be prepared to have them available as participants arrive. Some churches choose to furnish books for group members at no charge. Other churches choose to allow member to pay some or all of the cost of materials. Consider the possibility that members may take the study more seriously if they share in the cost. Try to provide scholarships for anyone who is unable to purchase the book.
- Set up a chalkboard or marker board for use during the session.
- Arrange the room in a way that is conducive for group interaction and sharing.
- Prepare a schedule with meeting times (and places, if they will be changing throughout the study) and your contact information (phone number, email) to pass out at the end of the session.

During the Session

- Ask each group member to make a nametag for herself.
- Distribute books to group members. Ask someone in the group to help collect money.
- Ask members to read the Introduction and About the Study sections silently as everyone arrives.
- Ask for volunteers to share a time in their lives when they didn't get what they ordered.
- Read John 10:10 aloud: " 'The thief does not come except to steal, and to kill, and to destroy. I have come that they may have life, and that they may have it more abundantly' " (NKJV).
- Remind the group that the original Greek word for *abundantly* is *perissos* (per-is-sos') and means *beyond measure, superabundant, or exceedingly abundantly above.* Reread the verse and substitute "exceedingly abundantly above" for "more abundantly."
- Ask volunteers to share what commonly hinders them from experiencing the abundant life.
- Ask participants to share what they hope to get out of the study.
- Ask the women to share the differences between "just a life" and the abundant life. Draw a column for each on your marker board or chalkboard and list the differences as members voice them. Ask them to be specific. Ask the women to share what it would take for them personally to be in the abundant life category.

- Distribute the schedule your prepared before the session.
- Close the session by praying for the group as you begin this study together.

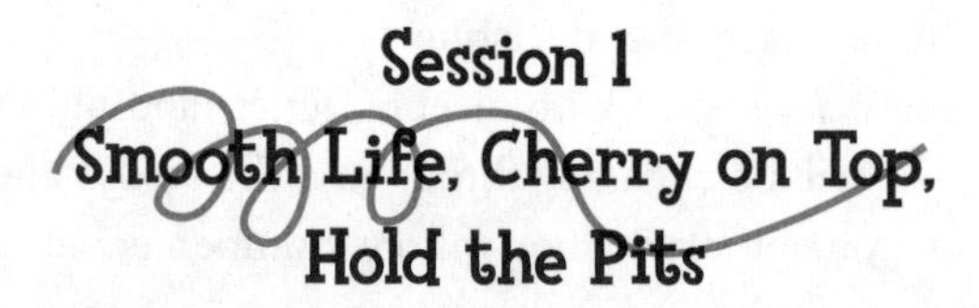

Session 1
Smooth Life, Cherry on Top, Hold the Pits

Before the Session

- Gather markers and materials for making nametags for all persons attending.
- If there are new group members, make sure they each get a book.
- Arrange the room in a way that is conducive for group interaction and sharing.

During the Session

- Ask each group member to make a nametag for herself.
- Ask the women to share real-life situations of adversity (concerning themselves or someone they know) that left them wondering if the abundant life could be possible.
- Have the women offer popcorn responses to the following statement: *It would be difficult for me to experience the abundant life if…*
- Say, *In day 1, we discussed how God used Joseph's dream to hint that He would someday use him in a mighty way. Do you believe God desires to use you in a mighty way? Ask volunteers to share a time when God hinted He would use them in a mighty way.*
- Turn to page 12. Ask volunteers to share the circumstances of the unforeseen trial they listed.
- Ask the women if they were able to apply the transforming truth that the Lord was with them.
- Reread the excerpt by Oswald Chambers on page 13. Ask, *Does the notion that "God is there," come as naturally as breathing when adversity hits?*
- Turn to page 14. Ask for volunteers to share a trial that knocked the wind out of them.
- Share: *The Lord was with Joseph and he prospered. If* prosper *means* push forward, *what hope does that offer us during times of adversity?*
- Ask members to turn to page 15. Review the list of trials Joseph experienced. Have the women share how someone might react to the same trials today.
- Ask, *When you experience a trial, are you more inclined to rush to the phone or the throne?*
- Remind the women that Ephraim means " 'God has made me fruitful in the land of my suffering' " (Gen. 41:52). Ask, *Does God desire to make us fruitful in the land of our suffering?*
- Have someone share a time of adversity when they chose bitter rather than better. Then have someone share a time of adversity when they chose better rather than bitter.
- In closing, ask participants to share in groups of two or three what truth(s) God laid on their hearts during session 1.
- Close in prayer, asking God to help each group member remember that He is with them and desires to prosper them in times of adversity. Ask Him to help everyone choose better instead of bitter during times of adversity.

Session 2
One Prince Charming, Well-Done, Please

Before the Session
- Gather markers and materials for making nametags for all persons attending.
- If there are new group members, make sure they each get a book.
- Set up a chalkboard or marker board for use during the session.
- Arrange the room in a way that is conducive for group interaction and sharing.

During the Session
- Ask each group member to make a nametag for herself.
- Have the women share a favorite fairy tale they recall from childhood with a prince and a "happily ever after" ending. Ask them what qualities they admired in the prince.
- Have volunteers share a favorite romantic scene in a movie that left them wishing it would play out in real life.
- Ask, *What are some ways the world sends us the message that a man will complete us and make us happy? Have you bought into this message? If so, how?*
- Remind the group that the Greek word for *fullness* or *fill* is *pleroo* (play-ro'-o); which means *to level up (a hollow), or to finish or complete.* Ask them if a man is capable of fully finishing or completing a woman.
- Ask, *How might most women define perfect love?* Write the answers on the chalkboard or marker board.
- Review the verses on page 29. Ask the women which ones were especially meaningful to them and why.
- Ask the women to support the idea that the story of redemption is the greatest love story ever told.
- Have volunteers share their thoughts regarding the description of the drama sketch on pages 30-31. Ask how they feel about the statement that they are no better than the drunk driver in the sketch.
- Ask for volunteers to share their answers to the question on page 33, "Why do most people invest their energy in human relationships rather than a relationship with Jesus?" in light of the fact that only God can provide everlasting and eternal love.
- Have women share the advice they would give a new bride regarding communication (p. 34), and how this advice might contribute to a thriving relationship with God.
- Have group members respond to the idea (day 5) that Jesus Christ is our one perfect love. Reread Psalm 73:25. Ask them to share common hindrances to Christ becoming their "everything."
- In closing, ask participants to share in groups of two or three what truth(s) God laid on their hearts during session 2.
- Close in prayer, asking God to help the women view Him as their one perfect love. Thank Him for leveling up the hollow places in our lives and completing us.

Session 3
I'm in a Hurry, So Make It to Go!

Before the Session
- Set up a chalkboard or marker board for use during the session.
- Arrange the room in a way that is conducive for group interaction and sharing.

During the Session
- Ask the women to share whether they think most people live at a "dine in" or "to go" pace.
- Ask volunteers to share their opinion of why people are so busy, in spite of all the time-saving devices available today.

- Ask members to share the differences between the rat race and the right race. Draw a column for each on your marker board or chalkboard and list the differences as members call them out. Ask, *Why do many Christians choose to run in the rat race in spite of the fact they have qualified for the right race? What is the first key factor in the pursuit to be a champion in the right race? What does it involve?*
- Reread the verses on page 44 with their associated benefits. Ask volunteers to share which verses were especially meaningful to them.
- Ask, *What is the second key factor in the pursuit to be a champion in the right race? What does it involve?*
- Ask for volunteers to answer, *What does it take to be more of a Mary than a Martha and cultivate the habit of sitting at the feet of Jesus?*
- Ask, *What is the third key factor in the pursuit to be a champion in the right race? What does it involve? What part does prayer play in equipping us to run the race at God's pace? What is the fourth key factor in the pursuit to be a champion in the right race? What does it involve?*
- Remind group members that to focus on the finish line, it is essential to view heaven as a positive notion. Have them share their answer to the question on page 51, "When you think of heaven, what comes to mind?"
- Have the women respond to the story of the father/son team who competed in the Ironman Triathlon. Ask, *How do you relate to the son in the story?*
- In closing, ask participants to share in groups of two or three what truth(s) God laid on their hearts during session 3.
- Close in prayer, asking God to help the women in your group commit to run the race as champions. Ask God to help each member run the race at His pace.

Session 4
I'll Have What She's Having, Please

Before the Session

- Set up a chalkboard or marker board for use during the session.
- Arrange the room in a way that is conducive for group interaction and sharing.

During the Session

- Have the women share names of women they admire and wish to emulate.
- Have the women discuss in small groups of two to three what areas of their lives they most commonly compare to other women: husband, personality, physical qualities, money, children, etc.
- Ask volunteers to share what area they most commonly struggle with in comparing themselves to others from their small-group discussions.
- Ask for volunteers to share their experiences of times when something was not fair and they came out on the short end.
- Review the parable Jesus told of the landowner and the workers (p. 59). Ask, *Did you find the actions of the landowner fair or unfair?*
- Ask, *How might wanting for little because you are accustomed to getting what you want produce negative implications in our relationship with God?* (day 3)
- Ask for volunteers to share a time when they wanted something yet hesitated to run it past God because they knew in their hearts that He might say no.
- Ask, *What can we learn from the Israelites about focusing more on our way than God's way?*
- Discuss the story of the lepers that Jesus healed (p. 69). Ask group members if they relate more to the leper who returned to thank Jesus or one of the ones who failed to show gratitude.

- Give the women 2 minutes to list as many things as possible for which they are grateful. At the end of the time period, ask them to share a few of the things they listed. Write their responses on your marker board or chalkboard.
- Ask, *What is the ultimate source of an attitude of gratitude? In other words, for what should we be most thankful?*
- Ask women to share practical ways to cultivate the habit of remembering all God has done. Ask them what they would say to express gratitude if they stood before the rugged cross of our Savior.
- In closing, ask participants to share in groups of two or three what truth(s) God laid on their hearts during session 4.
- Close in prayer, asking God to help group members resist the temptation to compare themselves and their circumstances to others. Ask Him to help each woman develop an attitude of gratitude, rooted in the incomparable love of the cross.

Session 5
I'll Take the #1 with Extra Me-O

Before the Session

- Arrange the room in a way that is conducive for group interaction and sharing.

During the Session

- Ask the women to brainstorm and think of people who have heroically put the needs of others before their own.
- Put the women into pairs and give each pair a fashion magazine. Have them tear out articles or ads that send a "me first" message. Allow time for each pair to share one item they picked with the large group.
- Share, *God wants us to love ourselves, but how does that factor into loving God and others?*
- Ask, *Why is it so difficult to focus on our own faults and weaknesses rather than the shortcomings of others?*
- Ask group members, *Can you think of a time when you chose Jesus over the world? What were the circumstances?*
- Look over the verses on page 78 regarding our relationship with the world. Ask volunteers to share which verses were especially meaningful to them.
- Review the introduction to day 3. Discuss which areas cause each of you an ongoing struggle.
- Read Ephesians 4:21-32. Ask, *Which characteristics of the "old self" and "new self" do you struggle with most?*
- Ask, *Why is it important to be in the habit of confessing your sins to God?*
- Read 1 John 2:3-6. Ask volunteers to respond to the verse.
- Ask, *If we are dead to sin, why do we continue to sin?* (p. 86) *Why do you think so many Christians struggle with coming to the end of themselves and dying fully to sin?*
- Ask participants to share in groups of two or three what truth(s) God laid on their hearts during session 5.
- Close in prayer, asking God to give group members the desire to die fully to sin and offer themselves as living sacrifices to God.

Session 6
I'll Have the All-You-Can-Eat Buffet

Before the Session

- Arrange the room in a way that is conducive for group interaction and sharing.

During the Session

- Put the women in pairs and have them role-play the following scenario: Two acquaintances strike up a friendly conversation about religion. One woman says, "You don't really believe that Jesus is the only way to heaven, do you?" The other woman, a Christian, defends her faith. Allow time for several pairs to share their role play with the large group.
- Ask the women to respond to the statement, "All major religions have the same basic tenets." Ask them how Christianity is different from other major world faiths.
- Ask, *If Jesus were to ask you today, "Who do people say the Son of Man is?" how would you answer?*
- Ask for responses to the quote by C.S. Lewis on page 92.
- Ask volunteers to share a time they had the opportunity to share their faith with a skeptic and questions or comments presented by the skeptic that they found challenging. Ask them, *Overall, were you equipped to defend the Christian faith?*
- Discuss how the women felt about the Barna statistics regarding born-again Christians (pp. 93-94).
- Discuss how John 14:6 and Acts 4:12 refute the belief that many paths lead to heaven.
- Ask, *In the quest to be a good soldier of Christ, how might we do the work of an evangelist as we go about our day-to-day activities?*
- Ask participants to share in groups of two or three what truth(s) God laid on their hearts during session 6.
- Spend the remainder of the time discussing the self-assessment results on pages 102-103. Ask each of the women to pinpoint one of the six myths covered during the study in which they need improvement.
- Allow the women time to express how the study helped them in the pursuit of the abundant life. Commend them for their commitment to study God's Word.
- Read John 10:10 aloud: " 'The thief does not come except to steal, and to kill, and to destroy. I have come that they may have life, and that they may have it more abundantly' " (NKJV)
- Remind the women once more that the original Greek word for *abundantly* is *perissos* (per-is-sos') and means *beyond measure, superabundant, or exceedingly abundantly above.* The abundant life is worth the effort and pursuit.
- Close in prayer, thank God for your time together in this study and for the relationships the women have built. Ask God to help each member refuse to order off the world's menu and look to Christ alone in the quest to get a life.

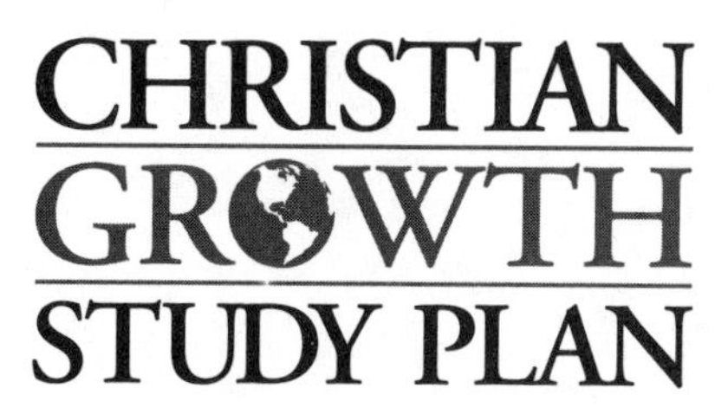

Preparing Christians to Serve

In the **Christian Growth Study Plan (formerly Church Study Course)**, *Get a Life!* is a resource for course credit in the subject area Christian Growth of the Christian Growth category of plans. To receive credit, read the book, complete the learning activities, show your work to your pastor, a staff member or church leader, then complete the following information. This page may be duplicated. Send the completed page to:

Christian Growth Study Plan
One LifeWay Plaza, Nashville, TN 37234-0117
Fax: (615)251-5067; Email: cgspnet@lifeway.com

For information about the Christian Growth Study Plan, refer to the Christian Growth Study Plan Catalog. It is located online at *www.lifeway.com/cgsp*. If you do not have access to the Internet, contact the Christian Growth Study Plan office (1.800.968.5519) for the specific plan you need for your ministry.

Get a Life! Debunking Six Myths in the Quest for Contentment
CG-0810

PARTICIPANT INFORMATION

Social Security Number (USA ONLY-optional)	Personal CGSP Number*	Date of Birth (MONTH, DAY, YEAR)
- -	- -	- -

Name (First, Middle, Last)	Home Phone
	- -

Address (Street, Route, or P.O. Box)	City, State, or Province	Zip/Postal Code

CHURCH INFORMATION

Church Name		
Address (Street, Route, or P.O. Box)	City, State, or Province	Zip/Postal Code

CHANGE REQUEST ONLY

☐ Former Name		
☐ Former Address	City, State, or Province	Zip/Postal Code
☐ Former Church	City, State, or Province	Zip/Postal Code

Signature of Pastor, Conference Leader, or Other Church Leader	Date

*New participants are requested but not required to give SS# and date of birth. Existing participants, please give CGSP# when using SS# for the first time. Thereafter, only one ID# is required. **Mail to:** Christian Growth Study Plan, One LifeWay Plaza, Nashville, TN 37234-0117. Fax: (615)251-5067.

Rev. 5-02